fishes of california and western mexico

1. *Rhamphocottus richardsoni* Guenther, the grunt sculpin, is one of the most prized aquarium fishes of the cool water areas of the eastern Pacific. Photo by Ken Lucas at Steinhart Aquarium.

by dr. warren e. burgess & dr. herbert r. axelrod

pacific
marine
fishes

book 8

Distributed in the UNITED STATES by T.F.H. Publications, Inc., 211 West Sylvania
Avenue, Neptune City, NJ 07753; in CANADA by H & L Pet Supplies Inc., 27 Kingston
Crescent, Kitchener, Ontario N2B 2T6; Rolf C. Hagen Ltd., 3225 Sartelon Street,
Montreal 382 Quebec; in ENGLAND by T.F.H. Publications Limited, 4 Kier Park,
Ascot, Berkshire SL5 7DS; in AUSTRALIA AND THE SOUTH PACIFIC by T.F.H.
(Australia) Pty. Ltd., Box 149, Brookvale 2100 N.S.W., Australia; in NEW ZEALAND by
Ross Haines & Son, Ltd., 18 Monmouth Street, Grey Lynn, Auckland 2 New Zealand; in
SINGAPORE AND MALAYSIA by MPH Distributors (S) Pte., Ltd., 601 Sims Drive,
03/07/21, Singapore 1438; in the PHILIPPINES by Bio-Research, 5 Lippay Street, San
Lorenzo Village, Makati Rizal; in SOUTH AFRICA by Multipet Pty. Ltd., 30 Turners
Avenue, Durban 4001. Published by T.F.H. Publications Inc., Ltd. the British Crown
Colony of Hong Kong.

TABLE OF CONTENTS

INTRODUCTION

The eastern Pacific region as covered by this volume extends from Alaska in the north to northern Chile in the south, almost the entire Pacific seaboard of the Americas. As such it includes a wide variety of tropical, temperate, and even coldwater fishes. The tropical zone is relatively narrow due to the direction of flow of certain ocean currents. In the Northern Hemisphere the major current involved flows past Alaska and Canada southward along the California coast before it starts to become warm enough to sustain a truly tropical fauna. In the Southern Hemisphere the current flows along the coast of Antarctica and then northward along the western shores of South America, where it does not become warm until off the very northwestern section of that continent.

The land mass of the Americas provides a formidable barrier between the eastern Pacific forms and the Caribbean or Atlantic forms, but this barrier was not always there. In relatively recent geological history the two faunas were able to mix, and a close affinity between the eastern Pacific and Caribbean faunas can be seen. Throughout this book there will be references to geminate or twin species; that is, a pair of species (one on each side of the Americas) that are so close morphologically that it is difficult to distinguish them, especially if their origin is not known. In many cases scientists do not believe many of these are distinct and thus consider both the Atlantic and Pacific forms as belonging to the same species. Other scientists maintain that they are distinct enough to warrant separate scientific names.

The tropical and temperate regions of the eastern Pacific are bordered on the west by the vast East Pacific Barrier. This is a broad stretch of very deep oceanic water that prevents shallow-water tropical and temperate forms from reaching the eastern Pacific from the Indo-Pacific and vice versa. A few shallow-water species with pelagic larvae that remain in the plankton for extended periods of time can and actually have made the crossing and are represented in the fauna of the eastern Pacific. The Moorish idol and the long-nosed butterflyfish are two examples of such species found in both the Indo-Pacific and the eastern Pacific.

The northern coldwater species are not so restricted, and many have distributions across the Bering Sea to the U.S.S.R. and Japan. In the south, however, there is no handy land mass before the Antarctic continent that could serve as a bridge for the exchange of coldwater forms between South America and Africa or Australia and New Zealand. It is interesting to note that the butterflyfish genus *Amphichaetodon* has two closely related species, one found off the coast of Chile and the other off the coasts of northern New Zealand and southeastern Australia. Perhaps some species are able to "island hop" across the Pacific, while others may take the colder route along the coast of Antarctica.

As usual, this series of books depends a great deal upon the photographers who supply us with photos of the appropriate fishes. In this volume we have had the great fortune to find two accomplished photographers who have specialized in different parts of the eastern Pacific, and we have utilized the talents of one of our good friends to cover a different section. Fishes from the northern colder waters (California coast and northward) were in the main photographed by Daniel W. Gotshall, whose work can be seen in many other publications. The Gulf of California (also known as the Sea of Cortez) was splendidly covered by Alex Kerstitch, who has also aided us in many additional ways. Finally, Dr. Gerald R. Allen went to Panama to photograph fishes there for us that helped to broaden the scope of the book considerably. Adding to these *in situ* photos were a large number of photos of fishes from the eastern Pacific that were at the time housed at the famous Steinhart Aquarium. The most prolific photographer of these aquarium fishes was Ken Lucas, whose excellent photos can be seen scattered throughout this book.

Canada

United States

Mexico

Pacific Ocean

Galapagos
Islands

1932

Family MYXINIDAE
HAGFISHES

The hagfishes, along with the lampreys, belong to a very primitive group of jawless fishes (class Agnatha) called cyclostomes, but they differ enough from the lampreys to be placed in their own order, the Myxiniformes. They are elongate, worm-like fishes with a suctorial mouth surrounded by several somewhat thickened barbel-like appendages and provided with two clusters of sharp teeth. Respiration is through a series of gill pouches. The skin is smooth and without scales and is provided with numerous mucous pores that produce so much mucus that a hagfish, when irritated, can turn the water in an aquarium into a slimy mess. Hagfishes are, therefore, sometimes referred to as slime eels. They are voracious scavengers, causing havoc with commercial fishermen who may find some of their catch rendered useless by the hags (they will actually bore into the body of a netted fish and eat it from the inside out).

2. Close-up of the mouth and barbels of a hagfish, *Eptatretus* sp., collected around Oregon. Photo by Ken Lucas at Steinhart Aquarium.

3. *Eptatretus stouti* (Lockington), the Pacific hagfish, in its typical coiled position in an aquarium. This species is fairly common and ranges from Alaska to Baja California. Photo by Ken Lucas at Steinhart Aquarium.

Hagfishes are cool- to coldwater fishes usually found in waters with temperatures below 12° or 13°C and at depths from about 30 meters to 1,000 meters. A hagfish burrows into soft muddy or clay substrates with only the tip of its head exposed as it waits for a scent in the current that will lead it to some food, for hagfishes are blind and can only locate food by smell. In an aquarium they will at times assume a coiled position, as seen in the accompanying photo.

Subclass ELASMOBRANCHII
SHARKS and RAYS

The sharks and rays are predominantly marine animals although some enter fresh water and a very few spend all their lives in fresh water. The estimated 800 species are currently divided into some 18 orders containing 29 families. They all have cartilaginous skeletons and are covered with small, tooth-like scales (dermal denticles or placoid scales). There are five to seven gill slits on each side (placed either laterally or ventrally). Male cartilaginous fishes (including chimeroids) have elongate copulatory organs called claspers at the inner posterior edge of each pelvic fin. Fertilization is internal, but the sharks and rays may be oviparous (laying eggs in cases), ovoviviparous (the eggs are retained in the oviduct until the young hatch), or truly viviparous (they bear living young that are nourished by a placenta-like structure while in the oviduct.)

The typical sharks have the usual shark-like shape and the gill slits are positioned on the side of the head. Rays have a very flattened head and body with the gill slits completely on the underside. The pectoral fins in rays extend forward and are attached to the head, resulting in a disc-like shape. There are intermediate forms such as the angel sharks, which are flattened like the rays but have their gill slits partly on the side of the head; their large pectoral fins are not attached to the head. Generally the angel sharks, as the name implies, are placed with the sharks and not the rays. On the other hand, the sawfishes and guitarfishes have somewhat shark-like bodies, but because their gill slits are located on the underside of the body, they are classified as rays.

4. The sevengill shark, *Notorynchus maculatus* Ayres, is easily recognized by its seven gill slits (count 'em). Some experts consider the eastern Pacific species to be a synonym of the more widely distributed *N. cepedianus*. Photo by Ken Lucas at Steinhart Aquarium.

5. *Heterodontus francisci* (Girard), the horn shark, is a nocturnal bottom-dwelling shark, solitary by nature, that may be found in rocky crevices or caves during the day. Photo by Daniel W. Gotshall at Catalina Island.

6. *Heterodontus* sp. (probably *H. francisci*—the spots may disappear in adults) about 1 meter long. A similar species also found in the Gulf of California (*H. mexicanus*) has low eye ridges, larger spots, and a light bar across the top of the head. Photo by Alex Kirstitch at Isla San Pedro Martir, Sonora, Mexico. Light spots in the photo are shrimp larvae.

7. *Ginglymostoma cirratum* (Bonnaterre), the nurse shark, sharing a cave with some soldierfish (*Myripristis leiognathus*) and a cardinalfish (*Apogon retrosella*). The nurse shark is found both in the eastern Pacific and western Atlantic. Photo by Dr. R. E. Thresher at Punta Pescadero, Gulf of California.

8. *Cetorhinus maximus* (Gunnerus), the basking shark, feeds by swimming in a slow circle with its mouth open, straining small planktonic animals through its gill rakers. Photo by Daniel W. Gotshall.

9. *Isurus oxyrinchus* Rafinesque, the shortfin mako (sometimes called the bonito shark), is a potentially dangerous shark. It is one of the fastest swimmers among sharks and is capable of leaps out of the water when hooked, making it a favorite of sports fishermen. Note the parasitic copepods on the dorsal fin. Photo by Alex Kerstitch, Baja California, Mexico.

10. *Cephaloscyllium ventriosum* (Garman), the swell shark, is more or less harmless. It can inflate its stomach with water (or air when out of water) and wedge itself into a crevice so that it is difficult or impossible to remove. Photo by Ken Lucas of a specimen from Monterey Bay at Steinhart Aquarium.

11. *Cephaloscyllium ventriosum* (Garman), juvenile, with more prominent white spots on its body. Photo by Daniel W. Gotshall, Isthmus Reef.

12. *Mustelus henlei* (Gill), the brown smoothhound, is recognizable from other members of the genus by the frayed rear edges of the dorsal fins. It feeds on a variety of fishes and invertebrates (crabs, shrimp, worms, sea squirts). Photo by Dr. Herbert R. Axelrod.

13. *Triakis semifasciata* Girard, the leopard shark, is often kept in home aquaria when small. Unfortunately, it grows too large (males to 1.5 meters, females to over 2 meters) to be kept very long. Photo by Aaron Norman.

14. A larger individual of the leopard shark. Although normally a strong-swimming wanderer, sometimes in schools, it will at times rest on the bottom as seen here. Photo of an individual from San Francisco Bay by Ken Lucas at Steinhart Aquarium.

15. *Squalus acanthias* Linnaeus, the spiny dogfish, a few days before birth. The spiny dogfish is ovoviviparous, with up to 20 young per litter. The spines preceding the dorsal fins are mildly toxic. Photo by Ken Lucas at Steinhart Aquarium.

16. *Squatina californica* Ayres, the Pacific angel shark, is flattened like a ray, but the large pectoral fins are not attached to the sides of the head as in the rays and the gill slits are in a notch at the rear of the head, not under the head as in rays. Photo by Daniel W. Gotshall.

17. *Rhinobatos productus* (Ayres), the shovelnose guitarfish, belongs to the most primitive rays, having the enlarged pectoral fins confluent with the head and the gill slits totally on the ventral side of the body. Photo by Ken Lucas at Steinhart Aquarium of an individual from Monterey Bay.

18. *Zapteryx exasperata* (Jordan & Gilbert), the banded guitarfish, has a range that extends from southern California to Panama. It prefers rocky areas. Photo of a 1-meter individual from Punta San Antonio, Sonora, Mexico, by Alex Kerstitch.

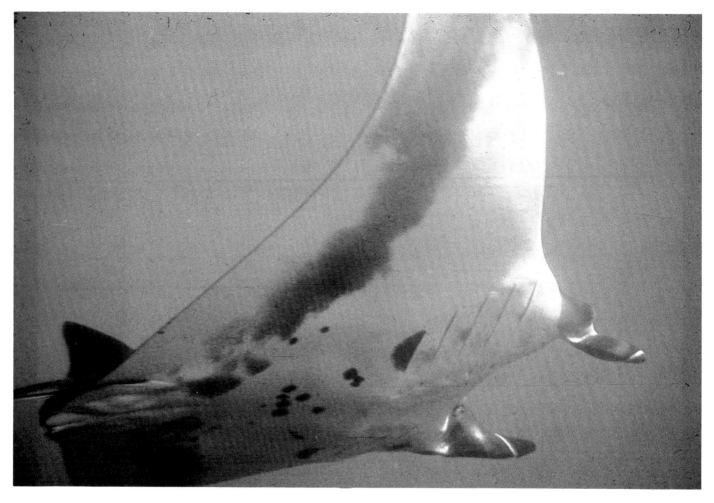

19. *Manta hamiltoni* (Newman), the Pacific manta, may possibly be identical with the more wide-ranging *Manta birostris*. This individual was estimated to be approximately 3½ to 4½ meters across. Photo by Alex Kerstitch at Isla San Pedro Martir, Sonora, Mexico.

20. *Platyrhinoidis triseriata* (Jordan & Gilbert), the thornback ray, receives its common name by virtue of the three rows of hooked spines on its back and tail. It is closely related to the guitarfishes. Photo by Daniel W. Gotshall at Santo Tomas, Baja California, Mexico.

21. *Urolophus concentricus* (Osburn & Nichols), the bullseye stingray, differs only in color pattern from *U. halleri* (below) and may eventually be proved to be synonymous with it. This individual is about 45 cm long. Photo by Alex Kerstitch at about 14 meters depth at Isla San Pedro Martir, Sonora, Mexico.

22. *Urolophus halleri* Cooper, the round stingray, is quite common off the California coast and is often stepped upon by bathers, resulting in nasty but almost always non-fatal wounds. This individual of about 0.75 meters is in the dark phase. Photo by Alex Kerstitch at about 6 meters deep at Isla San Pedro Nolasco, Sonora, Mexico.

23. *Torpedo californica* Ayres, the Pacific electric ray, swims by movements of the tail like a shark, rather than with undulations of the pectoral fins as do most other rays. This species feeds at night in rocky areas. Photo by Daniel W. Gotshall at Monterey Bay, California.

24. *Diplobatis ommata* (Jordan & Gilbert), the ocellated electric ray, has a very potent shock. This individual was about 20 cm in length. Photo by Alex Kerstitch at a depth of 12 meters at Isla San Pedro Martir, Sonora, Mexico.

Families MURAENIDAE, OPHICHTHIDAE, and CONGRIDAE
EELS

Of the three families of eels covered here, the best known are the moray eels of the family Muraenidae. Common rocky area or reef-dwelling eels of the tropics, the morays have muscular, slightly compressed bodies, well developed teeth (as almost anyone who has seen one can attest), no pectoral fins, and nearly round gill openings. Many are pleasingly patterned and have been kept in home aquaria in spite of their potential for mischief. Although most morays are less than 120 cm long, some do get quite large (more than 300 cm). During the day many morays remain in the rocks with only their heads sticking out; at night they come out of their holes and wander over the reef searching for food. The California moray, *Gymnothorax mordax*, is active at night, feeding on crustaceans, octopuses, and small fishes. The jewel moray, *Muraena lentiginosa*, has similar habits and may have a slightly venomous bite.

The snake eels or worm eels, family Ophichthidae, are nearly round in cross section and quite slender. They can usually be recognized by their naked tail tips, which are used for burrowing into the substrate. Small pectoral fins (at least in the West Coast species) and a lateral line are present. These are usually small eels (less than 90 cm), but a few species may grow to twice that length. They are tropical to subtropical bottom-dwelling eels, with some species extending into temperate waters. More than 200 species are known worldwide.

The conger eels (family Congridae) are generally gray or brown eels, sometimes with black-edged dorsal and anal fins. Pectoral fins are usually present, and the gill openings are slit-like. A lateral line is present. Although the teeth are well developed, there are no long canines like those in the moray eels. Many are predators on other fishes as well as invertebrates.

The garden eels (subfamily Heterocongrinae of Congridae) are burrowing forms that can be found in relatively dense "beds" or "gardens" in sandy areas. They can be seen with their heads in the water column and their tails in their burrows, picking at planktonic animals that are carried within their range by the water currents. They are said to be reasonably hardy in captivity.

25. *Gymnothorax castaneus* (Jordan & Gilbert), the Panamic green moray, is the largest moray eel in the Gulf of California, exceeding 1.8 meters in length. Photo of a 1.8-meter individual by Alex Kerstitch at 4.5 meters depth at Pulmo Reef, Baja California, Mexico.

26. *Gymnothorax panamensis* (Steindachner), the masked moray, is so-called because of the prominent black ring that encircles the eye. This species may extend across the southern Pacific to Lord Howe Island off Australia. Photo by Alex Kerstitch of a 28.6-cm specimen taken at 28 meters at Punta Doble, Bahia, San Carlos, Sonora, Mexico.

27. *Gymnothorax mordax* (Ayres), the California moray, feeds nocturnally on squid, crustaceans, and fishes. This species is said to live more than 30 years. Photo by Ken Lucas at Steinhart Aquarium.

28. *Muraena lentiginosa* Jenyns, the jewel moray, attains a maximum length of about a meter. This is a juvenile specimen (about 20 cm long and in its dark color phase) that was trawled at a depth of about 20 meters. Photo by Alex Kerstitch at Morro Colorado, Sonora, Mexico.

29. An adult jewel moray estimated to be close to a meter in length. It is unusual to be able to see this much of a moray's body during the daytime. Photo by Alex Kerstitch at a depth of about 9 meters at Cabo San Lucas, Baja California, Mexico.

30. *Muraena clepsydra* Gilbert, the hourglass moray, extends southward from the Gulf of California to Ecuador and the Galapagos Islands. This specimen, about a meter in length, was trawled from a depth of 40 meters. Photo by Alex Kerstitch at Morro Colorado, Sonora, Mexico.

31. *Quassiremus notochir* (Gilbert), the orange-banded snake eel, is not very often encountered. This specimen of 85 cm total length was collected at a depth of about 18 meters at Isla San Pedro Nolasco, Sonora, Mexico. Photo by Alex Kerstitch.

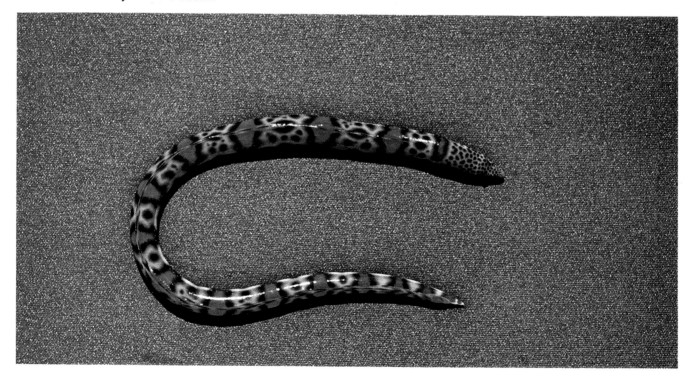

32. *Myrichthys maculosus* (Cuvier), the tiger snake eel, was known as *M. tigrinus* at one time, hence the common name. This individual is about 50 cm long. Photo by Alex Kerstitch at about 9 meters at Morro Colorado, Sonora, Mexico.

33. *Ophichthus* sp. (possibly *O. triserialis* (Kaup), the Pacific snake eel) with most of the body exposed. This is a rapid tail-first burrower, and in this photo part of the tail is already under the substrate. Without specimens to key out, snake eels are notoriously hard to identify. Photo by Dr. R. E. Thresher.

34. *Taenioconger canabus* Cowan & Rosenblatt, the Cape garden eel, was recently discovered and described from Isla Ceralbo. It has white halos around the anterior lateral line pores. Photo by Alex Kerstitch at a depth of 18 meters at Los Frailes, Baja California, Mexico.

35. Cortez garden eels come up out of their burrows to feed on the planktonic animals that drift by. At the approach of danger they disappear very quickly backward into their burrows. Photo by Alex Kerstitch at a depth of 15 meters at Isla San Pedro Martir, Mexico.

36. *Taenioconger digueti* Pellegrin, the Cortez garden eel, showing a closer view of the head. The colorless markings along the lateral line and the dark-colored minute pectoral fins are clearly visible. Photo by Alex Kerstitch at about 15 meters depth at Isla San Pedro Martir, Sonora, Mexico.

Families CLUPEIDAE and ENGRAULIDAE
HERRINGS AND ANCHOVIES

The herrings and anchovies are small, compressed, silvery fishes that lack a lateral line and have a single spineless dorsal fin, no adipose fin, and abdominal ventral fins. Most are schooling fishes that form a basic food supply for many of the larger predators whether they be fishes, birds, aquatic mammals, or other marine hunters. They usually inhabit shore waters of tropical and temperate seas, though some are abundant in quite cool water.

The herrings (family Clupeidae) generally have sawtoothed bellies with keels of scutes, deeply forked caudal fins, cycloid scales, and small mouths. They are plankton-feeders, straining food through their long, numerous gill rakers, and some species are provided with a pouch in which food particles are accumulated. The family contains in the neighborhood of 200 species.

The anchovies (family Engraulidae) are similar in many respects to the herrings but have characteristically long snouts that overhang large mouths, the upper jaws extending behind the eyes. The California species lack belly scutes, but many species have them. Many engraulids possess a distinct silvery lateral stripe, the rest of the body being more or less milky or transparent. The most common species on the West Coast is the northern anchovy, *Engraulis mordax*. It is round in cross section, whereas the other engraulids of the area are compressed.

37. *Clupea harengus pallasii* Valenciennes, the Pacific herring, is a very important commercial species. Fortunately it is very prolific, with a female able to lay up to 125,000 eggs. Photo by Dr. Gerald R. Allen of 30-cm individual at Steinhart Aquarium.

38. *Dorosoma petenense* (Guenther), the threadfin shad, is more commonly seen in fresh water, but it also extends into more brackish or marine situations in bays or harbors. Photo by Dr. Herbert R. Axelrod at Steinhart Aquarium.

39. *Opisthonema* sp., possibly *O. libertate* (Guenther), the deep-bodied thread herring, of about 7.5 cm length. Photo by Dr. Gerald R. Allen on the Pacific coast of Panama.

40. *Engraulis mordax* Girard, the northern anchovy, seen feeding on tiny planktonic animals (possibly newly hatched brine shrimp under aquarium conditions). Photo of individuals from Monterey Bay by Ken Lucas at Steinhart Aquarium.

41. A closer view of the northern anchovy showing the typical overhanging snout of the anchovies and the silvery lateral stripe. Photo by Dr. Gerald R. Allen at Steinhart Aquarium.

42. *Oncorhynchus kisutch* (Walbaum), the coho or silver salmon, is an anadromous species ascending rivers to spawn. It is wide-ranging, being distributed from Korea and Japan to Alaska and along the western American coast to Baja California. Photo by Dr. Gerald R. Allen of a 35-cm individual at Steinhart Aquarium.

43. *Salmo gairdneri* Richardson, the rainbow trout or steelhead, in its sea-run or "steelhead" phase. After two to three years at sea the steelhead will move up streams to spawn. Photo by Dr. Gerald R. Allen of a 38-cm individual at Steinhart Aquarium.

44. *Synodus* sp. This young individual of about 10 cm length was photographed on the Pacific coast of Panama at a depth of 5 meters by Dr. Gerald R. Allen.

45. *Porichthys margaritatus* (Richardson), the pearly spot midshipman, is easily recognized by its color pattern. The dorsal fin spots are distinctive, as are the white and blackish crescent-shaped spots below each eye. Photo of a 15-cm individual by Alex Kerstitch at Guaymas, Sonora, Mexico.

46. *Porichthys notatus* Girard, the plainfin midshipman, is common in bays on the California coast and forms an important part of the diet of seals and sea lions. Photo by Ken Lucas at Steinhart Aquarium.

47. The plainfin midshipman as it is usually seen, that is, almost completely buried in the substrate. Photo by Daniel W. Gotshall at a depth of about 18 meters.

48. *Tomicodon humeralis* (Gilbert), the Sonora clingfish, is endemic to and quite common in the upper Gulf of California. It is most active during daylight high tides, feeding on barnacles, limpets, and small crustaceans. Ventral side showing disc. Photo by Alex Kerstitch of a specimen from Puerto Lobos, Sonora, Mexico.

49. The dorsal aspect of the Sonora clingfish showing the striped pattern and pair of dark dorsal spots behind the head. Photo by Alex Kerstitch of a 5-cm individual from Puerto Lobos.

Family GOBIESOCIDAE
CLINGFISHES

Clingfishes are mostly small—one species grows to 36 cm and a couple to more than 15 cm, but most are smaller than 8 cm—tropical and temperate marine fishes (a few species are found in freshwater streams in Central America, the Caribbean, and Cocos Island). They have large thoracic adhesive organs that enable them to "cling" to objects. This adhesive organ or sucking disc is composed anteriorly of modified pelvic fins and posteriorly of a fold of skin. The head is usually broad and flattened, with the body tapering quickly to a rather slender tail, giving a typical clingfish the general appearance of a flattened tadpole. The dorsal fin lacks spines and is located far back on the body (the unrelated Liparidae, which also have sucking discs, have the dorsal fin in an anterior position.)

The clingfishes mostly inhabit shallow waters, including the intertidal zone, fastening to such objects as rocks, algae, and sea grasses, residing in burrows, or even living among the spines of sea urchins. The colors and color patterns often match the object upon which they are sitting, and they are therefore very hard to detect. The adhesive eggs are generally deposited upon some object with a reasonably smooth, flat surface such as a bivalve shell, blade of sea grass, or algal frond, and the parent or parents stand guard over them until they hatch. The color of the eggs varies depending upon the species but also may match the substrate to which they are attached. The number of eggs deposited depends upon the species involved and may vary from a low of ten to as many as 2500 or more. Major genera in the eastern Pacific include *Gobiesox*, *Rimicola*, and *Tomicodon*. For the family an estimate of about 100 species in 33 genera has been given.

The common species in the Gulf of California seem to sort themselves out ecologically, with *Gobiesox pinniger* preferring a cobble beach, *Tomicodon humeralis* the more difficult area of the reef platform (where temperature extremes and the threat of desiccation are present), and *T. boehlkei* the rock walls.

50. *Gobiesox adustus* Jordan & Gilbert, the Panamic clingfish, has the widest range of any of the eastern Pacific clingfishes, extending from Mexico to Ecuador. Photo of a 2.5-cm individual from Guaymas, Sonora, Mexico, by Alex Kerstitch.

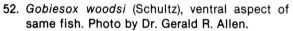

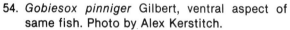

51. *Gobiesox woodsi* (Schultz), Woods' clingfish, from the dorsal aspect. Photo of a 2.5-cm specimen from Panama by Dr. Gerald R. Allen.

53. *Gobiesox pinniger* Gilbert, the tadpole clingfish, from the dorsal aspect. Photo of a 7.5 cm specimen from Puerto Lobos, Sonora, Mexico, by Alex Kerstitch.

52. *Gobiesox woodsi* (Schultz), ventral aspect of same fish. Photo by Dr. Gerald R. Allen.

54. *Gobiesox pinniger* Gilbert, ventral aspect of same fish. Photo by Alex Kerstitch.

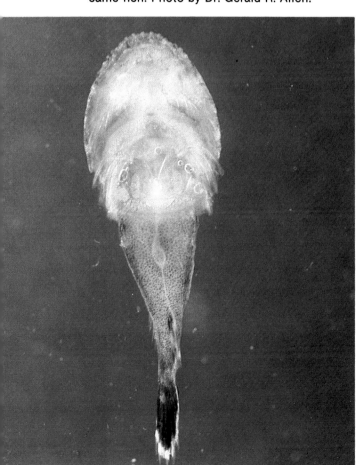

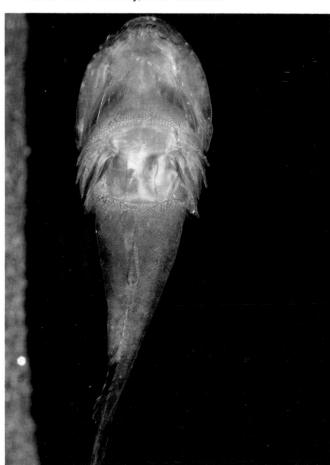

55. *Antennarius avalonis* Jordan & Starks, the roughjaw frogfish, may vary in color from lemon yellow through orange and red to black. Photo of a very young (2.1 cm total length) individual from Guaymas, Mexico, by Alex Kerstitch.

56. *Antennarius strigatus* (Gill), the bandtail frogfish, is most readily distinguished by the lack of the dorsal ocellus and the presence of the band on the tail. Photo of an individual from a depth of 18 meters at Isla San Pedro Nolasco, Sonora, Mexico, by Alex Kerstitch.

57. This specimen of *Antennarius strigatus* (Gill) is very pale. Note that the lure and second ray are folded back. Photo of a 5-cm individual collected at Isla San Pedro Nolasco, Sonora, Mexico, by Alex Kerstitch.

58. *Antennarius sanguineus* Gill, the sanguine frogfish, has been spawned in an aquarium. The canoe-shaped gelatinous egg raft was laid in two hours. Photo by Alex Kerstitch of a specimen collected at a depth of about 30 meters at Cabo San Lucas, Baja California, Mexico.

59. *Antennarius sanguineus* Gill from Panama. The range of this species extends from the central Gulf of California to Peru, including the Galapagos Islands. Photo of an 11.4-cm specimen from Panama by Dr. Gerald R. Allen.

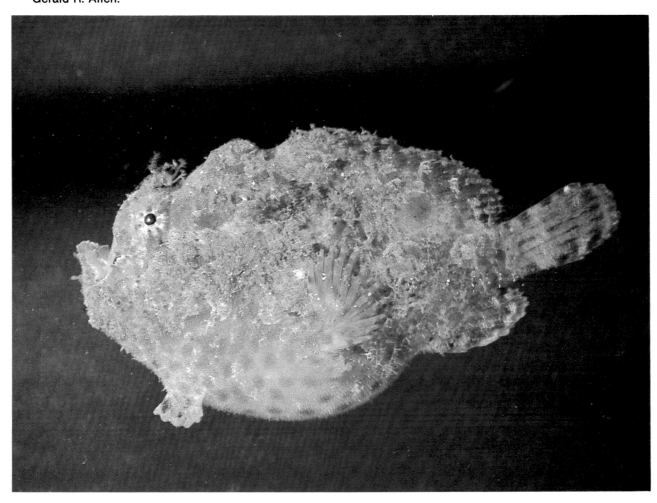

1960

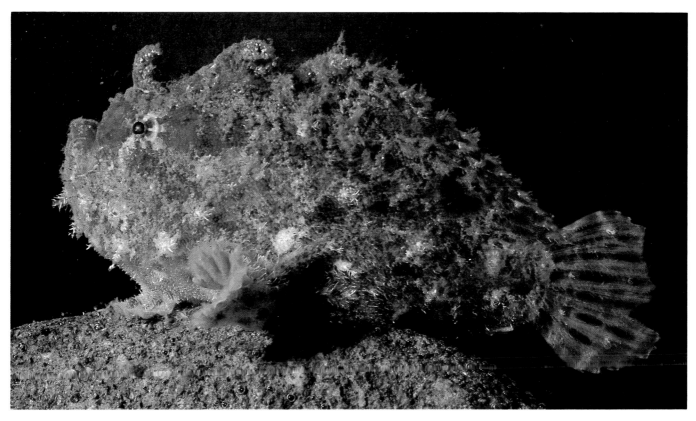

60. *Antennarius* sp., possibly also *A. sanguineus.* The shape, color, pattern, and surface growths all contribute to making it very difficult to spot this fish in its natural habitat among overgrown and encrusted rocks. Photo of a 7.5-cm individual from Panama by Dr. Gerald R. Allen.

61. *Zalieutes elater* (Jordan & Gilbert), the spotted batfish, is well marked with the two bull's-eyes on its back. It prefers a sandy bottom where it can be seen "walking" along on its arm-like pectoral fins. Photo of a specimen 10.7 cm total length from Morro Colorado, Sonora, Mexico, by Alex Kerstitch.

62. *Brosmophycis marginata* (Ayres), the red brotula, inhabits rocky areas from southeastern Alaska to the northern Gulf of California. Photo by Ken Lucas at Steinhart Aquarium.

63. *Ogilbia* sp. (probably a new species). This genus differs from *Brosmophycis* by having scaled cheeks. Photo of a 6-cm individual from Guaymas, Sonora, Mexico by Alex Kerstitch.

64. *Lepophidium prorates* (Jordan & Bollman), the Pacific blackedge cusk-eel, has dark edges to the dorsal and anal fins. This black edging is best seen in this photo at the anterior part of the dorsal fin. Photo of a 10-cm individual taken during a night dive off Punta Chivato, Baja California, Mexico, by Alex Kerstitch.

65. *Chilaria taylori* (Girard), the spotted cusk-eel, is usually active at night. It lives over sandy bottoms and is able to burrow tail-first into the sand. Photo by Daniel W. Gotshall at a depth of about 15 meters off the Monterey breakwater.

66. *Lycodes pacificus* Collett, the blackbelly eelpout, was formerly placed in the genus *Lycodopsis.* It inhabits mud bottoms over a range from the Gulf of Alaska to the Gulf of California. Photo of a 25-cm individual by Dr. Gerald R. Allen at Steinhart Aquarium.

67. A school of needlefishes, possibly *Strongylura exilis* (Girard), most approximately 20 cm in length, swimming just below the water's surface. Photo by Alex Kerstitch at Guaymas, Sonora, Mexico.

1964

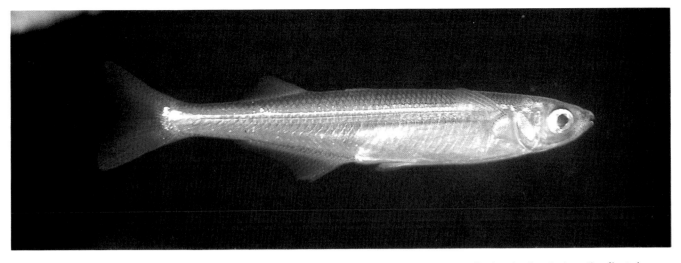

68. *Atherinops affinis* (Ayres), the topsmelt, is recognized by having the anal fin beginning below the first dorsal fin. This 7.5-cm individual was photographed at Steinhart Aquarium by Dr. Gerald R. Allen.

69. An *Atherinops affinis* more than twice the length of the above at 18 cm. Photographed at Steinhart Aquarium by Dr. Gerald R. Allen.

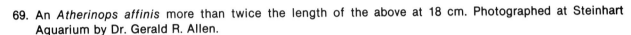

70. An almost fully grown topsmelt at about 30 cm. Photographed at Steinhart Aquarium by Dr. Gerald R. Allen.

Family HOLOCENTRIDAE
SQUIRRELFISHES and SOLDIERFISHES

Squirrelfishes and soldierfishes are usually nocturnal fishes of shallow tropical marine waters. The dorsal fin is deeply notched, with an anterior spiny portion and a posterior soft-rayed portion, and the eyes are usually large. The scales are quite rough, and there is a strong tendency toward a red (or some shade of red) coloration. Being nocturnal fishes, they generally remain hidden in darkened parts of the reef (caves, crevices, etc.) during the day and swim out over the reef at night searching for food. There are only about 70 species in the family included in approximately nine genera, with only a few species occurring in the eastern Pacific. A major division of the family into the soldierfishes (Myripristinae) and squirrelfishes (Holocentrinae) is readily observable through the presence of a strong preopercular spine in the genera of the subfamily Holocentrinae that is absent in the genera of the subfamily Myripristinae. Courtship is said to be accompanied by a series of clicking noises apparently produced by the well developed pharyngeal teeth. The eggs are pelagic, and a specialized spiny-nosed larva called a rhynchichthys develops.

The Panamic soldierfish, *Myripristis leiognathos,* is most commonly seen in small aggregations in shallow water at night foraging for food. During the day it aggregates in sheltered areas on the reef such as caves and crevices, often with other nocturnal species. This is a widely distributed species occurring from the Gulf of California to Ecuador.

The tinsel squirrelfish, *Sargocentron suborbitalis* (formerly *Adioryx suborbitalis*), also feeds at night but apparently does not form aggregations such as does the Panamic soldierfish. The primary food is crustaceans, which they capture in the splash zone in waters less than about 3 meters deep. This species also extends from the Gulf of California south to the coast of Ecuador, including most of the offshore islands.

71. *Sargocentron suborbitalis* (Gill), the tinsel squirrelfish, hiding in its cave during the day. At night it will emerge to feed on small crustaceans. Photo of a 15-cm adult taken by Alex Kerstitch at 3 meters depth at Guaymas, Sonora, Mexico.

72. *Myripristis leiognathos* Valenciennes, the Panamic soldierfish, aggregates in caves or under ledges during the day in fairly shallow water (less than 15 meters). Photo by Alex Kerstitch at about 6 meters depth at Pulmo Reef, Baja California, Mexico.

73. A "clinical" photo of *Myripristis leiognathos*. Soldierfishes, including those of the genus *Myripristis,* lack the prominent preopercular spine of the squirrelfishes. Photo by Dr. Gerald R. Allen of a 15-cm specimen from Panama.

74. *Aulorhynchus flavidus* Gill, the tubesnout, is a relative of the sticklebacks. It builds a nest in the kelp that is guarded by the male. Photo by Daniel W. Gotshall off the California coast.

75. *Fistularia commersoni* Rueppell, the reef cornetfish, usually assumes this blue-striped pattern while swimming, whereas when feeding or motionless it can quickly become barred or mottled. This individual is about 1 to 1½ meters long. Photo by Alex Kerstitch at a depth of 12 meters at Cabo San Lucas, Baja California.

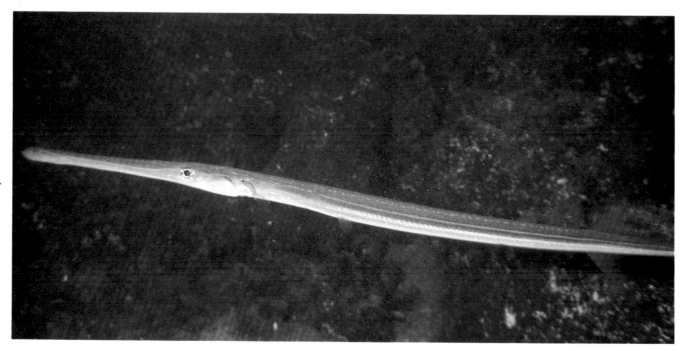

Family SYNGNATHIDAE
PIPEFISHES and SEAHORSES

Pipefishes and seahorses are predominantly shallow-water fishes occurring in tropical and temperate marine waters, although some species are known to occur in freshwater habitats. The bodies of both pipefishes and seahorses are encased in rigid bony plates forming rings, giving them an almost segmented appearance. Their snouts are generally tubular, with small, toothless mouths at the end. There is normally a small, rayed dorsal fin; pelvic fins are lacking. Pipefishes usually are supplied with small caudal fins, which seahorses lack. Males of both seahorses and pipefishes usually have brood pouches on their abdomens that may extend onto the tail segments; in many pipefishes, however, the actual pouch is absent. The female deposits her eggs into the pouch or attaches them to the underside of the male pipefish's body in the same general area where a brood pouch would occur. There the eggs are carried until *he* gives birth to living young, often going through many contortions in the process.

Syngnathids occur in a variety of habitats but seem to prefer shallow water where there is abundant vegetation. Of approximately 34 genera containing some 150 species of pipefishes and two genera containing about two dozen seahorses, only a single seahorse and about 15 or 16 pipefishes occur in the eastern Pacific.

The Pacific seahorse, *Hippocampus ingens*, has a range that extends from San Diego to Peru, favoring areas of patch reef where sea whips occur. It is commonly brought up in shrimp trawls in the Gulf of California.

The fantail pipefish, *Doryrhamphus excisus excisus*, is commonly found in pairs (male and female) in secluded parts of the reef. Like many nocturnal species, these fish are often seen in inverted positions in their hideouts. The brightly colored caudal fins are displayed when they are frightened or when they are defending their territory against conspecifics. The male is said to be able to incubate up to about 100 eggs at a time.

The bay pipefish, *Syngnathus leptorhynchus*, is more of a temperate species, occurring from Monterey Bay in California north to Alaska. It prefers areas where there is a good growth of eel grass.

76. *Hippocampus ingens* Girard, the Pacific seahorse, is the only seahorse known from the eastern Pacific. It is usually found associated with sea whips at depths of more than 10 meters. Photo by Alex Kerstitch at 18 meters at Isla San Nicolas, San Carlos, Sonora, Mexico.

77. *Doryrhamphus excisus excisus* Kaup, the fantail pipefish, usually occur in sexual pairs and defend their territories from others of their own kind. Photo by Alex Kerstitch at 3 meters depth at Cabo San Lucas, Baja California, Mexico.

78. This small pipefish (about 5 cm) was collected and photographed by Dr. Gerald R. Allen at Panama. It appears to be a species of *Micrognathus* from the Indo-Pacific and may be a stray.

79. *Syngnathus auliscus* (Swain), the barred pipefish, seems to prefer shallow bays and lagoons, where it occurs in eelgrass. Photo of a specimen 15 cm total length from Guaymas, Sonora, Mexico, at a depth of 6 meters by Alex Kerstitch.

80. *Syngnathus leptorhynchus* Girard, the bay pipefish, is quite common in bays, where it is found among the eelgrass. Photo by Ken Lucas of a number of specimens from Tomalas Bay, California, at Steinhart Aquarium.

81. *Syngnathus leptorhynchus* Girard, close-up of the head and snout. Snout length and number of body and tail rings are useful characters in identification of these pipefishes. Photo by Dr. Gerald R. Allen at Steinhart Aquarium.

1971

82. *Centropomus nigrescens* Guenther, the black snook, attains a length of up to a meter or so and has a range from Mexico to Panama. Photo by Alex Kerstitch.

83. *Morone saxatilis* (Walbaum), the striped bass, was transplanted from the eastern coast of the U.S. in the late 1800's and has become well established in western America, with a range from Barkley Sound, B.C., to northern Baja California. Photo by Ken Lucas at Steinhart Aquarium.

84. *Stereolepis gigas* Ayres, the giant sea bass, showing a close-up of the head. It is said that specimens live to an age of at least 70 years. Photo of a 1.4-meter individual by Dr. Gerald R. Allen at Steinhart Aquarium.

85. *Stereolepis gigas* is called the black sea bass, but giant sea bass seems more appropriate considering that it attains a length of 226 cm and a weight of over 227 kilos (500 pounds). Photo by Dr. Herbert R. Axelrod.

86. *Stereolepis gigas* young, as shown here, have a different color pattern than the adults shown on the previous page. Photo by Ken Lucas at the Steinhart Aquarium.

87. *Diplectrum pacificum* Meek & Hildebrand, the Pacific sand perch, can most readily be recognized by color pattern and the diverging spines at the angle of the preoperculum. Photo by Alex Kerstitch of a 10.5-cm specimen taken at Guaymas, Sonora, Mexico.

88. *Epinephelus (Dermatolepis) dermatolepis* Boulenger, the leather bass, juvenile with the typical barred pattern that makes it so attractive to aquarists. Photo by Aaron Norman.

89. These barred juveniles will seek shelter in spiny sea urchins, usually the diademid *Centrostephanus coronatus.* However, under aquarium conditions they will often take to other diademids as substitutes. Photo by Aaron Norman.

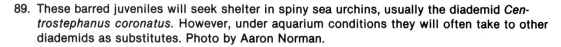

90. As the leather bass grows, its color changes drastically. Here is a young adult *Epinephelus dermatolepis* of about 25 cm in a cave at a depth of 30 meters. Photo by Alex Kerstitch at Cabo San Lucas, Baja California, Mexico.

91. A slightly larger leather bass with the head pattern considerably changed, as also is the caudal pattern. Photo by Dr. Herbert R. Axelrod at the Steinhart Aquarium.

92. An adult *Epinephelus dermatolepis* showing additional changes in the color pattern. Photo by Dr. E. S. Hobson.

93. *Epinephelus (Promicrops) itajara* (Lichtenstein), the jewfish, is another grouper that grows to enormous size. This one, over 2 meters in length, is estimated to weigh between 600 and 700 pounds. Photo by Alex Kerstitch at a depth of 21-22 meters at Baja California, Mexico.

94. *Epinephelus (Epinephelus) labriformis* (Jenyns), the flag cabrilla, has a range from Mexico to Peru and is said to be a solitary predator. This fairly young individual is only about 13 cm in length. Photo by Dr. Gerald R. Allen at Panama.

95. A much smaller flag cabrilla of approximately 7.5 cm with a quite similar pattern although differing in details. Photographed at a depth of 15 meters by Alex Kerstitch at Isla San Pedro Nolasco, Sonora, Mexico.

96. Fish-eye view of *Epinephelus (Alphestes) multiguttatus* (Guenther), the Pacific mutton hamlet or Pacific guaseta. This individual of about 20 cm in length was photographed at a depth of 18 meters by Alex Kerstitch at San Carlos, Sonora, Mexico.

97. *Epinephelus (Alphestes) multiguttatus* in lateral view, showing the body pattern. This species is very difficult to tell from the mutton hamlet, *E. afer* (which is found in both the Atlantic and East Pacific), the two species differing mostly in details of the color pattern. Photo by Dr. R. E. Thresher at Cabo Pulmo, Gulf of California.

98. *Epinephelus (Cephalopholis) panamensis* (Steindachner), the Panama graysby, is a secretive fish keeping to caves and crevices along rocky coastlines. This is an adult about 30 cm in length, photographed at a depth of 15 meters by Alex Kerstitch at Isla San Pedro Martir, Sonora, Mexico.

99. *Epinephelus panamensis* has been reported to attack and try to eat fishes near its own size in captivity, making aquarists a bit wary about keeping one. Photo by Dr. R. E. Thresher at Loreto, Gulf of California.

100. *Epinephelus (Epinephelus) analogus* Gill, the spotted cabrilla, is another voracious predator, with fishes and crustaceans forming the bulk of its diet. Photo by Emerson, from Walford's *Marine Game Fishes.*

101. *Epinephelus (Epinephelus) niveatus* (Valenciennes), the snowy grouper, is another of those species occurring in warm waters of both the western Atlantic and eastern Pacific. This is a juvenile photographed by U. Erich Friese.

102. *Epinephelus (Epinephelus) acanthistius* (Gilbert), the Gulf coney, is a fairly common bottom-fish at depths greater than 50 meters in the Gulf of California. Shown is a 50-cm specimen photographed by Emerson, from Walford's *Marine Game Fishes.*

103. An unusually large individual of the leopard grouper, appearing to approach the maximum size for the species. Photo by Alex Kerstitch of a 1-meter specimen estimated at 45 kilograms at 18 meters depth at Isla San Pedro Martir, Mexico.

104. *Mycteroperca rosacea* (Streets), the leopard grouper, feeds voraciously on herrings and anchovies soon after sunset. During the day aggregations can be seen near rocky prominences and are apparently relatively inactive. Photo by Dr. Gerald R. Allen of a 50-cm individual from the Gulf of California at Steinhart Aquarium.

105. *Mycteroperca rosacea* is sometimes seen in a "golden" phase (only about 1% of the population undergoes this transformation) and may also be referred to as the golden grouper. Photo of an individual about 50 cm long by Alex Kerstitch at Isla San Pedro Martir, Sonora, Mexico.

106. *Mycteroperca prionura* Rosenblatt & Zahuranec, the sawtail grouper, at this size (30 cm) is covered with roundish reddish brown spots. With growth the spots become smaller and more numerous. Photo by Dr. Gerald R. Allen at Steinhart Aquarium.

107. *Liopropoma fasciatum* Bussing, the banded bass, is a relatively deep-water species that was only recently discovered and was described in 1980. Photo of a 15-cm individual captured at 54 meters depth by Alex Kerstitch near Scripps Institution.

108. *Liopropoma fasciatum* of approximately 12.5 cm length in its natural habitat at a depth of about 67 meters. Photo by Alex Kerstitch at Cabo San Lucas, Baja California, Mexico.

109. *Paralabrax maculatofasciatus* (Steindachner), the spotted sand bass, will remain near cover close to the bottom from shallow water (intertidal) to more than 60 meters. It preys on fishes and crustaceans during daylight hours. Photo by Ken Lucas at Steinhart Aquarium.

110. *Paralabrax nebulifer* (Girard), the barred sand bass, prefers sandy bottoms in the vicinity of rocks. Its depth range is considerable, from shallow water to depths of over 180 meters. Photo by Dr. Gerald R. Allen at the Steinhart Aquarium.

111. *Paralabrax auroguttatus* Walford, the goldspotted sand bass, is easily recognized by its multitude of gold-colored spots covering the head, body, and fins. Photo by Emerson, from Walford's *Marine Game Fishes.*

112. *Paralabrax loro* Walford, the parrot sand bass, has a deeper body than the other species and is found more at intermediate depths in the lower Gulf of California. Photo by Emerson, from Walford's *Marine Game Fishes.*

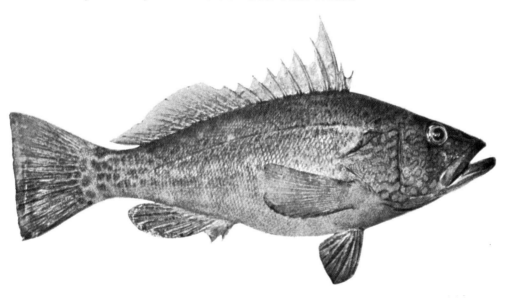

113. *Paralabrax clathratus* (Girard). The kelp bass, as its common name implies, is found in or around the kelp beds. It is said that breeding males develop a dusky orange lower jaw. Photo by Ken Lucas at Steinhart Aquarium.

114. *Paranthias colonus* (Valenciennes), the Pacific creole-fish, commonly occurs in small aggregations down to 60 meters. Photo of a pair of adults (30 cm) at 9-12 meters depth by Alex Kerstitch at Isla San Pedro Martir, Sonora, Mexico.

115. The white spots on the side and the bright red pectoral axil make this species easily identifiable. The Caribbean *P. furcifer* is very similar, and the two species may be synonymous. Photo by Ken Lucas at Steinhart Aquarium.

116. Color variety of an adult *Paranthias colonus* (spawning colors?). Photo by Alex Kerstitch at a depth of 15 meters at Cabo San Lucas, Baja California, Mexico.

117. *Hemanthias peruanus* (Steindachner), the splittail bass, is a deep-water form that is rarely encountered. Photo by Daniel W. Gotshall of a specimen from Baja California, Mexico.

118. *Serranus fasciatus* Jenyns, the barred serrano, is a solitary predator occurring on patch reefs down to about 60 meters depth. Photo of a 13-cm individual at 5 meters depth by Dr. Gerald R. Allen at Panama.

119. *Serranus fasciatus* of almost the same size (12.5 cm) but from a different locality than the individual on the opposite page. Photo at a depth of 15 meters by Alex Kerstitch at Isla San Pedro Nolasco, Sonora, Mexico.

120. A juvenile barred serrano of approximately 5 cm length at a depth of about 15 meters. After laboratory acclimation, juveniles were able to withstand temperatures down to 9.4°C. Photo by Alex Kerstitch at Sonora, Mexico.

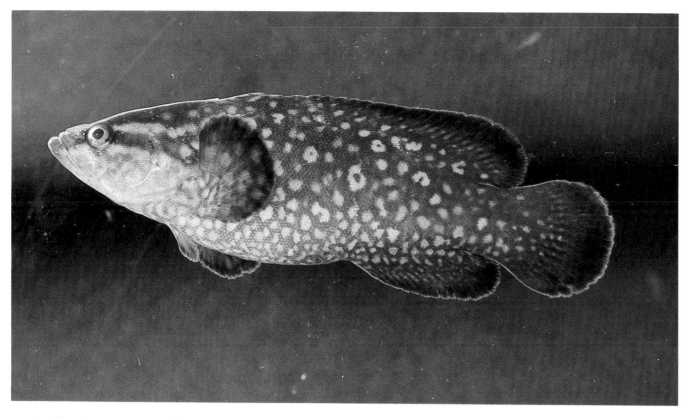

121. *Rypticus nigripinnis* Gill, the blackfin soapfish, has only two dorsal fin spines and attains a length of about 20 cm. In an aquarium it is very secretive, remaining hidden a great deal of the time. Photo by Dr. Gerald R. Allen of a 7.5-cm specimen from Panama.

122. *Rypticus bicolor* (Valenciennes), the Cortez soapfish, has three dorsal fin spines and attains a length of 30 cm. It is less timid in the aquarium than *R. nigripinnis* but, like other soapfishes, secretes a mucus when agitated and could thus be a dangerous tank inhabitant. Photo of an 18-cm individual by Dr. Gerald R. Allen at Panama.

123. *Pristigenys serrula* (Gilbert), the popeye catalufa, is a nocturnal fish that usually occurs at greater depths than cardinalfishes and squirrelfishes (to more than 75 meters). Photo by Daniel W. Gotshall of a specimen from Baja California.

124. *Pristigenys serrula* about 15 cm long. In an aquarium the light should be subdued and there should be plenty of hiding places (rock caves, etc.) provided. Photo by Alex Kerstitch at Scripps Aquarium.

125. *Apogon retrosella* (Gill), the barspot cardinalfish, is readily recognized by the black bar and spot against the red background. Even the young of this species have the characteristic markings. Photo of a 10-cm individual at 10 meters depth by Alex Kerstitch at Guaymas, Sonora, Mexico.

126. *Apogon pacifici* Herre (formerly *A. parri* Breder), the pink cardinalfish, ranges from Mexico to Peru and inhabits depths to at least 60 meters. Photo by Dr. R. E. Thresher at Juncalito, Gulf of California.

127. *Apogon pacifici* is easily distinguishable from the barspot cardinalfish by lacking the peduncle spot and having a much reduced sub-dorsal bar on its back. Photo of a specimen of 7.6 cm from Isla San Pedro Nolasco, Sonora, Mexico, by Alex Kerstitch.

128. *Apogon pacifici* is nocturnal and frequents caves or other dark places during the day. It is possibly a smaller species than the others in the East Pacific. This photo was taken in its typical habitat at a depth of 14 meters by Alex Kerstitch at Isla San Pedro Nolasco, Sonora, Mexico.

129. *Apogon dovii* (Guenther), the tailspot cardinalfish, differs from the other species of cardinalfishes on these pages by possessing only the round spot on the caudal peduncle. This 7.5-cm specimen was collected on the ocean side of the Perlas Archipelago, Panama, at a depth of 3-5 meters. Photo by Dr. Gerald R. Allen.

130. The tailspot cardinalfish has a range that extends from Mazatlan, Mexico to Peru. Here it shares its cave or ledge with a pipefish, *Doryrhamphus excisus.* Photo by Dr. Gerald R. Allen of a 5-cm individual at Panama.

131. *Caulolatilus princeps* (Jenyns), the ocean whitefish, inhabits offshore rocky reefs and banks from Vancouver Island to Peru. Photo by Daniel W. Gotshall.

132. This ocean whitefish was estimated to be about 65 cm in length (the maximum size for the species is said to be a little over 100 cm). Photographed at Steinhart Aquarium by Dr. Gerald R. Allen.

133. *Trachurus symmetricus* (Ayres), the jack mackerel, is a pelagic species often seen in large schools, even when young. Photo by Daniel W. Gotshall off San Benitos Island.

134. *Caranx sexfasciatus* Eydoux & Souleyet, the Indo-Pacific horse-eye jack, is one of those species whose range extends from the east coast of Africa to the eastern Pacific. Photo by Dr. Gerald R. Allen at Steinhart Aquarium.

135. *Caranx caninus* Guenther, the Pacific crevalle jack, and *Caranx caballus* Guenther, the green jack, schooling together at Punta Pescadero, Gulf of California, Mexico. The green jack is the less deep-bodied fish. Photo by Dr. R. E. Thresher.

136. *Selene brevoorti* (Gill), the Mexican lookdown, has a very unusual shape. Seen in broadside it presents a very large surface area, but if it is seen head-on it is so thin it virtually disappears. Photo of a specimen 10.7 cm long from Morro Colorado, Sonora, Mexico, by Alex Kerstitch.

137. *Trachinotus rhodopus* (Gill), the gafftopsail pompano, occurs in large schools over inshore sandy areas as well as in reef and rocky areas. It is readily recognized by the elongate fins and lateral bars. Photo of a 30-cm individual (closest to camera) taken by Alex Kerstitch at a depth of 3 meters at Guaymas, Sonora, Mexico.

138. *Nematistius pectoralis* Gill, the roosterfish, is the only species in its family (Nematistiidae). The distinctive elongate dorsal spines represent the rooster's "comb." Photo of a 36-cm specimen trawled at a depth of 10 meters at Morro Colorado, Sonora, Mexico, by Alex Kerstitch. Although adults exceed a meter in length, they look almost exactly like this juvenile in shape and pattern.

139. *Seriola dorsalis* (Gill), the California yellowtail, is now referred to as *S. lalandei dorsalis,* the common yellowtail. *S. lalandei* has a nearly worldwide distribution, the *dorsalis* subspecies extending from southern Canada to Chile. Photo by Ken Lucas at Steinhart Aquarium.

140. *Coryphaena hippurus* Linnaeus, the dolphin, is a pelagic game fish rarely photographed underwater in its natural habitat. It feeds on pelagic fishes, squids, and crustaceans. Photo of a 1-meter specimen taken at 10 meters depth off Baja California, Mexico, by Alex Kerstitch.

141. *Hoplopagrus guentheri* Gill, the barred pargo, is a nocturnal predator. Juveniles are commonly seen in shallow patch reefs around seaweed. Photo of a juvenile about 4 cm in length at Guaymas, Sonora, Mexico, by Alex Kerstitch.

142. *Lutjanus peru* (Nichols & Murphy), the Pacific red snapper or huachinango, is one of the deep-water snappers that are fished commercially. This specimen was taken by handline from a depth of about 90 meters at San Carlos, Sonora, Mexico. Photo by Alex Kerstitch.

143. *Lutjanus argentiventris* (Peters), the yellow snapper, is a relatively common snapper that feeds on small fishes, octopuses, and crustaceans. It is also said to be able to enter fresh water. Photo of a 60-cm individual taken at a depth of 9-12 meters at Guaymas, Sonora, Mexico, by Alex Kerstitch.

144. *Lutjanus guttatus* (Steindachner), the spotted rose snapper, is generally associated with sandy bottoms. It is readily recognized by the large black spot below the dorsal fin and often has horizontally arranged yellow to brownish stripes on the side. Photo of a 7.5-cm specimen from Panama by Dr. Gerald R. Allen.

145. Larger specimens of the spotted rose snapper may be faded as seen here but may become darker at a moment's notice depending upon the mood of the fish. Photo of an adult about 50 cm in length by Alex Kerstitch.

146. *Lutjanus viridis* (Valenciennes), the blue-and-gold snapper, is one of the more colorful snappers of the eastern Pacific. Photograph of a 30-cm individual at Cabo San Lucas, Baja California, Mexico, by Alex Kerstitch.

147. A pair of snappers, *Lutjanus viridis* (striped) and *L. argentiventris* (plain), at Cabo San Lucas, Baja California, Mexico. In the lower background is *Haemulon sexfasciatum.* Photo by Alex Kerstitch.

Family GERREIDAE
MOJARRAS

The mojarras are small, usually silvery, compressed fishes of mostly tropical to warm-temperate marine waters, although some are commonly found in brackish to even fresh waters. They are schooling fishes most often seen in inshore waters over sand or mud bottoms but may also occur in rocky areas where there are open sandy spots. The mouth is characteristically highly protrusible and is used to feed on invertebrates that may be buried in the sand. The dorsal and anal fins fold back into grooves formed by scaly sheaths. The tail is forked. Worldwide there are an estimated 40 species.

The spotfin mojarra, *Eucinostomus argenteus*, has a distribution that includes both the western Atlantic (New Jersey to Rio de Janeiro) and the eastern Pacific (southern California to Peru). It commonly inhabits shallow inshore areas, including bays, where there are sandy shores. The Pacific flagfin mojarra, *Eucinostomus gracilis*, is so-called because of the black and white pattern of its dorsal fin. It occurs in aggregations (loose schools) of one dozen to about four dozen individuals in shallow inshore areas over sandy or muddy bottoms. This includes open coastal regions, bays, inlets, and even estuaries with decreased salinities. The maximum size is about 20 cm. The food of the Pacific flagfin mojarra consists of various benthic invertebrates, including polychaete worms, molluscs, crustaceans, and even bryozoans. This and most other species of mojarras can easily be captured with the use of beach seines.

Although the mojarras are said to readily adapt to life in captivity, they are usually passed over for fishes that are more colorful.

148. *Eucinostomus gracilis* (Gill), the Pacific flagfin mojarra, is so-called because of the dark black spot (flag) at the tip of the dorsal fin. It occurs mostly in shallow inshore areas. Photo by Dr. Gerald R. Allen of a 15-cm individual at Steinhart Aquarium.

149. *Anisotremus taeniatus* Gill, the Panamic porkfish, is almost a dead ringer for the Atlantic porkfish. Such species pairs occur many times in many different families. Photo of an individual about 25 cm long at 18 meters depth by Alex Kerstitch at Los Frailes, Baja California, Mexico.

150. A school of *Anisotremus taeniatus.* Note how the shoulder bar has faded considerably in most of these individuals. Photo of 30-35 cm long individuals at a depth of 18 meters by Alex Kerstitch at Cabo San Lucas, Baja California, Mexico.

151. *Haemulon flaviguttatum* Gill, Cortez grunts, also tend to form schools or aggregations over rocky or reefy areas. They move offshore at night to feed. Photo of approximately 25-cm individuals at a depth of 6 meters by Alex Kerstitch at San Agustin, Sonora, Mexico.

152. *Anisotremus davidsoni* (Steindachner), the sargo, is easily distinguished by the single black bar below the anterior part of the dorsal fin. It is commonly seen near kelp beds over rocks or among rocks mixed with sand bottoms. Golden individuals also occur. Photo by Dr. Herbert R. Axelrod at Steinhart Aquarium.

153. *Haemulon sexfasciatum* Gill, the graybar grunt, has a distinctive pattern of yellowish and brownish gray bars. It ranges from the Gulf of California to Panama. Photo of an 80-cm individual taken at a depth of about 12 meters by Alex Kerstitch at Guaymas, Sonora, Mexico.

154. A school of graybar grunts over the edge of a rocky area. Such schools are said to disperse at dusk as individuals go their own way in search of food. Photo at a depth of 10 meters by Alex Kerstitch at Isla San Pedro Nolasco, Sonora, Mexico.

155. *Calamus brachysomus* (Lockington), the Pacific porgy, is mostly silvery in color as shown, but it can change to a mottled pattern very quickly. Photo of an individual about 45 cm long by Alex Kerstitch at Isla San Pedro Nolasco, Sonora, Mexico.

156. *Genyonemus lineatus* (Ayres), the white croaker, is an inshore species that is an important sports and commercial fish. Photo by Ken Lucas at Steinhart Aquarium.

157. *Roncador stearnsi* (Steindachner), the spotfin croaker, is readily recognizable by the large blackish blotch at the pectoral fin base. Adults feed primarily on clams, crabs and other crustaceans, and marine worms. Photo by Ken Lucas at Steinhart Aquarium.

158. *Umbrina roncador* Jordan & Gilbert, the yellowfin croaker, occurs mostly in shallow sandy areas where it feeds on small fishes and invertebrates. Note the short chin barbel. Photo by Ken Lucas at Steinhart Aquarium.

159. *Equetus viola* (Gilbert), the rock croaker, undergoes drastic pattern changes with growth. Shown here are very young juveniles of about 2.5 cm in length. Photo by Alex Kerstitch at a depth of about 4½ meters at Morro Colorado, Sonora, Mexico.

160. A rock croaker of about 6 cm length (more than twice the size of the above specimens) with a more striped pattern. Photo at a depth of 4½ meters by Alex Kerstitch at Punta Colorado, Sonora, Mexico.

161. An adult *Equetus viola* of about 30 cm with a fully adult pattern. Note also the changes in the shape of the dorsal fin. Photo by Alex Kerstitch at a depth of about 18 meters at Isla San Pedro Nolasco, Sonora, Mexico.

162. *Mulloidichthys dentatus* (Gill), the Mexican goatfish, occurs in small schools in rocky inshore areas. It is easily recognized by the yellow lateral stripe. Photo of approximately 30-cm individuals taken by Alex Kerstitch at a depth of 20 meters at Cabo San Lucas, Baja California, Mexico.

163. *Pseudupeneus grandisquamis* (Gill), the bigscale goatfish, is a warm-water species occurring from the Gulf of California to Chile, with a single specimen collected from the warm outflow of a nuclear power plant in California. Photo of an 11.4-cm specimen from Morro Colorado, Sonora, Mexico, by Alex Kerstitch.

164. *Girella nigricans* (Ayres), the opaleye, usually has two pale spots below the dorsal fin, but as seen in the photos on this page there may be only one (or none in some large specimens). Photo by Dr. Herbert R. Axelrod at Steinhart Aquarium.

165. The opaleye occurs around kelp beds and rocky areas, feeding on seaweed and occasionally small invertebrates. Photo by Ken Lucas at Steinhart Aquarium.

166. *Hermosilla azurea* Jenkins & Evermann, the zebra perch or zebraperch, is recognizable by the barred pattern plus the presence of a dark spot at the pectoral base and another (usually blue) at the posterior edge of each opercle. Photo by Daniel W. Gotshall at San Benito Island.

167. *Girella simplicidens* Osburn & Nichols, the Gulf opaleye, has a restricted distribution, occurring only in the Gulf of California, where it is much more common in the northern part. Photo by Dr. R. E. Thresher at Bahia de Los Angeles, Gulf of California, Mexico.

168. *Kyphosus analogus* (Gill), the blue-bronze chub, is a metallic blue with some bronzy stripes along the sides (it is sometimes called the striped sea chub). The fish at the edge of the photo is a zebra perch. Photo by Daniel W. Gotshall at San Benito Island.

169. *Kyphosus elegans* (Peters), the Cortez chub, is an herbivorous species but will dine on plankton and benthic invertebrates when the opportunity arises. The Atlantic geminate, *K. sectatrix,* is very similar. Photo by Alex Kerstitch at 3 meters depth at Isla Farallon, Sinaloa, Mexico.

170. *Medialuna californiensis* (Steindachner), the halfmoon, is another herbivore. It feeds primarily on seaweeds but also takes small invertebrates in rocky areas and around kelp beds. Photo by Ken Lucas at Steinhart Aquarium.

Family KYPHOSIDAE
SEA CHUBS, NIBBLERS,
and HALFMOONS

The family Kyphosidae at present includes three groups of fishes that were formerly considered separate families, i.e., the sea chubs or rudderfishes (now considered subfamily Kyphosinae), the nibblers (now considered subfamily Girellinae), and the halfmoons (now considered subfamily Scorpinae). They are usually compressed, oval-shaped fishes with small mouths provided with incisor-like teeth most commonly arranged in a single main row. All feed on benthic algae, small invertebrates, and plankton, the method of feeding providing at least one of the groups with its common name, the nibblers. The name rudderfishes stems from the habit of these fishes of following ships, whereas the halfmoons were named for the shape of their caudal fins. Worldwide there are approximately 30 species contained in some 15 genera. Although most species grow to only about 60 cm in length, at least one species attains a length of 90 cm.

The opaleye, *Girella nigricans,* occurs in dense schools in the California kelp beds in the spring and can be identified by the presence of two light spots on its back. The Gulf opaleye, *G. simplicidens,* has three or four such spots. Both species browse on algae and occasionally supplement their diet with invertebrates. As nibblers almost continuously peck at other fishes, they are generally not welcome as aquarium fishes.

The zebra perch, *Hermosilla azurea,* is similar in aspect to the opaleye but is distinguishable by the presence of a bright blue spot on the gill cover. It inhabits shallow inshore areas where it is commonly seen in schools with the Pacific sergeant major, *Abudefduf troschelii.* The halfmoon, *Medialuna californiensis,* may form small aggregations or occur as solitary individuals in the water column of rocky areas or areas where the growth of kelp is luxuriant. Like many of the other species, the diet includes seaweeds and small invertebrate animals.

Family EPHIPPIDAE
SPADEFISHES

Spadefishes are highly compressed fishes with deep, almost circular bodies that occur in most tropical waters but with an occasional incursion into temperate waters. Most of the 14 or 15 species are less than 50 cm in length, although some species may attain lengths in excess of 90 cm. The spinous dorsal fin may or may not be separated from the soft portion, and the latter often has the anterior rays prolonged in large adults, sometimes exceedingly so. The anal fin may also have the anterior soft rays prolonged to such an extent that they correspond in shape to the soft dorsal, creating a symmetry of sorts. The spadefishes are usually silvery in color, often with crossbars of black that may intensify or fade depending upon the mood of the fish. Young spadefishes may be quite dark in color and/or blotched so that they commonly resemble floating dead leaves. Their behavior of floating motionless on their sides in shallow water enhances this mimicry. They become lighter as they grow,

eventually assuming the silvery color of the adults. The young may also commonly be seen in brackish inshore areas. The spadefish mouth is small, and the diet usually includes small sessile invertebrates or shellfish of various kinds.

Only two species of spadefishes occur in the eastern Pacific: the Pacific spadefish, *Chaetodipterus zonatus*, and the Panama spadefish, *Parapsettus panamensis*. The Pacific spadefish is a common schooling fish with a range that extends from San Diego to Peru. It is reported to attain a length of more than 60 cm, although individuals greater than about 30 cm are not common. Juveniles are cryptically colored and are sometimes captured by the use of beach seines. Stomach contents of the Pacific spadefish have included crustaceans, polychaete worms, sponges, tunicates, gorgonians, anemones, molluscs, and even algae. The closely related Panama spadefish is found from Guaymas to Peru but is more of an offshore species than the Pacific spadefish. Unlike the Pacific spadefish, its dorsal spines are short and free and the last is the longest.

171. *Chaetodipterus zonatus* (Girard), the Pacific spadefish, is one of two species of spadefishes in the eastern Pacific, the other being *Parapsettus panamensis. Parapsettus,* however, has free dorsal fin spines with the last one longest; *C. zonatus* has dorsal spines with membranes and the third is longest. Photo by Dr. Herbert R. Axelrod at Steinhart Aquarium.

172. Juvenile Pacific spadefish are very dark in color. With age they become a basic silver with blackish bars. These bars may fade in murky water or over light-colored sand but increase in intensity over darker backgrounds such as reefs. Photo by Alex Kerstitch of 60-cm individuals at about 15 meters at San Carlos Bay, Sonora, Mexico.

173. *Chaetodipterus zonatus* is a schooling fish, as are almost all members of the family. This is another member of an Atlantic/Pacific species pair, the one from the Atlantic in this case being *C. faber.* Photo by Dr. R. E. Thresher at Punta Pescadero, Gulf of California.

174. *Chaetodon falcifer* Hubbs & Rechnitzer, the scythe butterflyfish, is one of the deeper-water species of butterflyfish, inhabiting depths between 12 and 150 meters. Photo by Al Engasser.

175. The scythe butterflyfish in its natural habitat some 75 meters deep. Also seen are a passer angelfish (behind butterflyfish) and blue-and-yellow chromis. Photo by Alex Kerstitch at Cabo San Lucas, Baja California, Mexico.

176. *Chaetodon humeralis* Guenther, the East Pacific banded butterflyfish, in its natural habitat. Butterflyfishes often pair as seen in this photo. It has been seen mingling with schools of small *Chaetodipterus zonatus* over open sand areas. Photo by Alex Kerstitch at 15 meters depth at Guaymas, Sonora, Mexico.

177. *Chaetodon humeralis* is a wide-ranging species, occurring from southern California to Peru. It is common at depths of 3 to 12 meters around rocky areas. Photo by Dr. Herbert R. Axelrod.

178. A number of Indo-Pacific species have ranges that extend to the eastern Pacific. One such species is *Forcipiger flavissimus* Jordan & McGregor, the long-nosed butterflyfish. Shown is a 15-cm individual photographed by Alex Kerstitch at a depth of 11 meters at Cabo San Lucas, Baja California, Mexico.

179. *Amphichaetodon melbae* Burgess & Caldwell, the narrow-barred butterflyfish, has as its closest relative a species on the southeastern Australian and New Zealand coasts. This species is known only from the San Felix Islands off Chile. Photo by Wayne Baldwin.

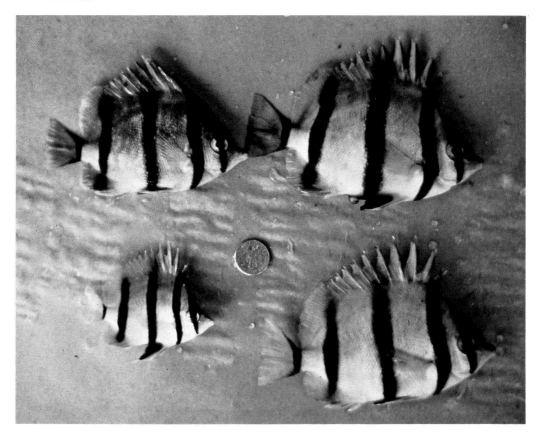

180. *Pseudochaetodon nigrirostris* (Gill), the black-nosed butterflyfish, aggregates at particular spots on the reef to which fishes come to be cleansed of parasites by them. For this reason it is also commonly called "el barbero." Photo by Alex Kerstitch at a depth of 10 meters at Cabo San Lucas, Baja California, Mexico.

181. The black-nosed butterflyfish has a wide range, occurring from the Gulf of California to Panama and the Galapagos Islands. It inhabits depths of from 6 to 12 meters. Photo by Ken Lucas at Steinhart Aquarium.

182. The diet of *Pseudochaetodon nigrirostris* consists chiefly of small invertebrates (including the parasites it picks) and some algae. Photo by Dr. Gerald R. Allen at Steinhart Aquarium.

183. *Holacanthus clarionensis* Gilbert, the Clarion angelfish, undergoes color changes with growth. Shown here is a small juvenile with a number of vertical blue stripes. Photo by Al Engasser.

184. With growth the blue stripes begin to weaken, as does the eye band. This individual would still be called a juvenile. Photo by Ken Lucas at Steinhart Aquarium.

185. As a subadult, *Holacanthus clarionensis* retains only traces of the juvenile pattern. Photo by Al Engasser.

186. A fully adult Clarion angelfish approximately 45 cm in length. Although occurring on the Mexican coastline, this species is more common at Clarion Island in the Revillagigedos, from which it received its common name. Photo by Alex Kerstitch at Cabo San Lucas, Mexico.

187. *Holacanthus passer* Valenciennes, the passer angelfish, also undergoes great changes in color pattern from juvenile to adult. Shown here is a very small juvenile, as can be seen by the hands surrounding it. Photo taken by Alex Kerstitch at a tidepool at Morro Colorado, Sonora, Mexico.

188. A slightly larger juvenile passer angelfish showing a generally lighter coloration, especially posteriorly. Note that the white stripe that will remain throughout the life of the fish is evident very early. Photo by Alex Kerstitch at Bahia San Carlos, Sonora, Mexico.

189. A 13-cm subadult shows both adult and juvenile color features as far as color pattern is concerned. The changes that this species goes through are very reminiscent of those of the Caribbean species of *Holacanthus (ciliaris* and *isabelita). Photo by Dr. Gerald R. Allen at Steinhart Aquarium.

190. This nearly fully grown adult passer angelfish has not only developed its full color pattern, but the dorsal and anal fins have become somewhat elongated. Photo by Dr. Gerald R. Allen at Steinhart Aquarium.

191. A *Holacanthus passer* adult about 25 cm long in its natural habitat. Females tend to be smaller than males and maintain a specific territory. Photo by Alex Kerstitch at about 5 meters depth at Cabo del Pulmo, Baja California, Mexico.

192. *Pomacanthus zonipectus* (Gill), the Cortez angelfish, at this size might at first glance be confused with Atlantic *Pomacanthus* juveniles. Photo by Alex Kerstitch of a 2.5-cm juvenile at a depth of 6 meters at San Agustin, Sonora, Mexico.

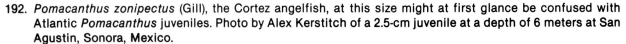

193. At 6 cm a few light blue lines start to appear on the Cortez angelfish juvenile, immediately differentiating it from the Atlantic species. Photo by Alex Kerstitich of an individual collected at about 5 meters at Morro Colorado, Sonora, Mexico.

194. The increasing number of blue lines can be seen in this 7.5-cm individual of *Pomacanthus zonipectus*. Juveniles are highly territorial like their Atlantic cousins, and two to a tank are sure to lead to disastrous fighting. Photo by Aaron Norman.

195. At this stage of its development, *Pomacanthus zonipectus* is starting to show some adult color pattern through the still prevalent juvenile pattern. The juvenile diet contains more vegetable matter (algae) than that of the adult, and they are facultative cleaners. Photo by Dr. Herbert R. Axelrod.

196. A fully adult Cortez angelfish of about 25 cm length with no trace of the juvenile color pattern. Adults are said to range widely over the reef as solitary individuals, pairs, or loose aggregations. Photo by Alex Kerstitch at a depth of 5-6 meters at Morro Colorado, Sonora, Mexico.

197. An adult *Pomacanthus zonipectus.* The Cortez angelfish ranges from the Gulf of California to Peru. Maximum size is about 46 cm, but the average size is closer to 25-30 cm. Photo by Ken Lucas at Steinhart Aquarium.

Family EMBIOTOCIDAE
SURFPERCHES

There are close to two dozen species of surfperches, most of which (19 to 21 species) may be found in the area from Alaska to Baja California (the other two species occur in Japan and Korea). All are marine fishes with the exception of *Hysterocarpus traski*, the tule perch, which inhabits the Sacramento River. A second species, *Cymatogaster aggregata*, may wander into brackish or even fresh water with no ill effects. The surfperches are compressed, with a more or less elliptical shape, and the dorsal fins are continuous, with no notch between the spinous and soft portions. They range in size from about 10 to 50 cm and may be plain silvery, barred, striped, or brightly colored. As suggested by their common name, most species occur in inshore areas around the surf on both sandy and rocky shores, although at least one species, the pink seaperch (*Zalembius rosaceus*), occurs in water to more than 200 m depth and a few prefer kelp beds or tide pools. The surfperches are among the few marine families that give birth to living young (viviparous), with as few as three to at least more than 100 per litter. Internal fertilization is practiced, the male being provided with a small, tubular intromittent organ at the front end of the anal fin. Most surfperches become sexually active almost immediately, the first copulation occurring very soon after birth. As in other truly viviparous animals, the young are nurtured by the mother internally.

Both the barred surfperch, *Amphistichus argenteus*, and the redtail surfperch, *A. rhodoterus*, are reported to be popular with sports fishermen. The barred surfperch gives birth to anywhere from a few to more than 100 young over 4 cm in length after a gestation period of five months. It is common not only in surfy areas but may also be caught in rocky areas and around piers. The kelp surfperch, *Brachyistius frenatus*, is so-called because it is almost always associated with kelp and feeds primarily on crustaceans that are associated with the giant kelp. The

198. *Amphistichus argenteus* Agassiz, the barred surfperch, is a common species along sandy coasts in the surf. It feeds on invertebrates, the favorite being sand crabs. Photo by Ken Lucas at Steinhart Aquarium.

199. *Amphistichus rhodoterus* (Agassiz), the redtail surfperch, is a more northerly ranging species, extending from Vancouver Island, B.C., to Monterey Bay, California. It also prefers surfy areas of sand beaches along the coast. Photo by Daniel W. Gotshall at Trinidad, California.

200. *Amphistichus rhodoterus* usually has all its fins reddish in color, especially the caudal fin, hence the common name. Photo by Ken Lucas, Steinhart Aquarium.

shiner surfperch, *Cymatogaster aggregata*, is perhaps the most commonly caught surfperch and is used for food by sports fishermen. It forms loose schools or aggregations along the coast and is said to be attracted to steam generating power plants, where thousands are destroyed in the intake pipes each year. Shiner perch feed on a variety of items, but crustaceans and algae seem to head the list; they in turn are fed upon by other fishes, birds, marine mammals, and even crabs.

Black surfperch, *Embiotoca jacksoni*, may have as many as 60 embryos 5 cm long (although females around 23 cm averaged 13 (5 to 26)) that are usually born in the spring or summer months. The walleye surfperch, *Hyperprosopon argenteum*, was observed mating. The pair swam together, matching turn for turn a few feet off the bottom. If the female stopped the male displayed in front of her with his snout tilted upward and his fins spread. Actual copulation occurred with the fish tilted toward one another to bring the

201. *Brachyistius frenatus* Gill, the kelp surfperch, prefers to inhabit kelp beds, where it feeds on small crustaceans. It is also said to be a cleaner. Photo by Daniel W. Gotshall.

202. *Cymatogaster aggregata* Gibbons, the shiner perch, usually occurs in loose schools or aggregations around eelgrass beds and pilings in shallow water. It also enters brackish or even fresh water. Photo by Ken Lucas at Steinhart Aquarium.

203. *Embiotoca lateralis* Agassiz, the striped surf-
     perch, has a range from southeastern Alaska
     to northern Baja California. It inhabits rocky
     areas and kelp beds to a depth of about 20
     meters. Photo by Daniel W. Gotshall.

204. *Embiotoca lateralis* (striped fish) and *Damalichthys vacca* (barred fish) in a kelp bed. The
     striped surfperch has narrow reddish orange and blue stripes. Photo by Daniel W.
     Gotshall, Todos Santos, Baja California, Mexico.

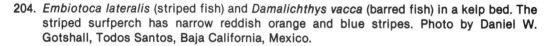

205. *Embiotoca jacksoni* Agassiz, the black surfperch, usually has about nine dark bars on
the side and sometimes a black "mustache"
as seen in this individual. Photo by Daniel W.
Gotshall of a fish in its natural habitat.

206. An adult black surfperch with the bars faded. This species is seen most often in rocky areas near kelp and
rarely in surfy areas, in spite of its common name. It is also known as butterlips or black seaperch. Photo by
Ken Lucas at Steinhart Aquarium.

207. A juvenile black surfperch. The range of the species is from northern California to northern Baja California. Photo by Ken Lucas at Steinhart Aquarium.

208. *Hyperprosopon argenteum* Gibbons, the walleye surfperch, often occurs in schools. It inhabits surfy areas of open sand beaches but is also found around rocks and piers. Photo by Daniel W. Gotshall off Catalina Island, California.

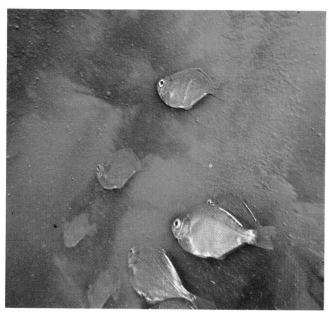

anal areas into close proximation. Intruding males were met with a charge by the courting male and usually fled the scene.

The rainbow surfperch, *Hypsurus caryi*, is a little over 30 cm long and is one of the more colorful surfperches, as the common name suggests. Its pattern of blue and orange markings on a silvery background makes this species a true candidate for the home aquarium. One of the smallest species is the dwarf surfperch, *Micrometrus minimus*, with a length of less than 8 cm. It occurs in rocky areas, including breakwaters and jetties, as well as among seaweeds near the rocky areas. Young are generally smaller than in other species but still are 2.5 cm long. The rubberlip surfperch, *Rhacochilus toxotes*, is one of the largest species of surfperches, attaining a length of almost 50 cm. The common name refers to the large, thick, pinkish white lips that are said to become so large in some individuals that they actually droop.

209. *Hyperprosopon ellipticum* (Gibbons), the silver surfperch, is found from southern Canada to northern Baja California, mostly in sandy, surfy areas. It attains a maximum length of about 27 cm. Photo by Ken Lucas at Steinhart Aquarium.

210. *Hypsurus caryi* (Agassiz), the rainbow surfperch, is one of the most colorful of the surfperches, showing a great deal of orange and blue on the body and black spots in the fins. Photo by Ken Lucas at Steinhart Aquarium.

211. The rainbow surfperch in its natural habitat, rocky shores often along the edges of kelp beds. It occurs at depths of up to 40 meters. Photo by Daniel W. Gotshall at Monterey, California.

212. *Hypsurus caryi* has a rather restricted range, being known from northern California to northern Baja California, thus roughly only along the California coast. Photo by Dr. Herbert R. Axelrod at Steinhart Aquarium.

213. *Micrometrus aurora* (Jordan & Gilbert), the reef surfperch, has a golden stripe along its side with emerald green above and silvery below. It feeds on algae and associated invertebrates. Photo by Dr. Gerald R. Allen at Steinhart Aquarium.

214. *Micrometrus minimus* (Gibbons), the dwarf surfperch, is quite small as the common name implies. It is usually less than 7.5 cm in length, but the maximum size is said to be 16 cm. Photo by Ken Lucas at Steinhart Aquarium.

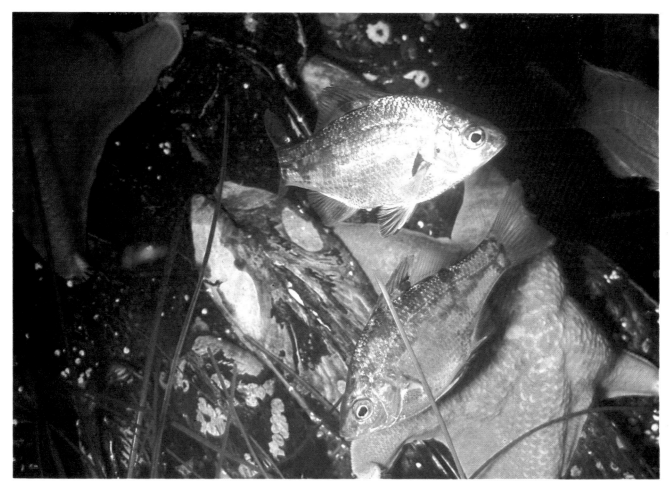

215. *Phanerodon atripes* (Jordan & Gilbert), the sharpnose surfperch, is a comparatively rare species that is common only in Monterey Bay, where this photo was taken. It attains a length of almost 30 cm. Photo by Daniel W. Gotshall.

216. *Phanerodon furcatus* Girard, the white surfperch, is most easily distinguished by the black line at the base of its dorsal fin. The similar sharpnose surfperch has blackish anal and pelvic fins and a reddish body. Photo by Ken Lucas at Steinhart Aquarium.

217. *Damalichthys vacca* Girard, the pile surfperch, is also known under the name *Rhacochilus vacca.* It is fairly large (to about 45 cm) and feeds on hard-shelled invertebrates such as crabs, molluscs, and even barnacles. Photo by Ken Lucas at Steinhart Aquarium.

218. *Rhacochilus toxotes* Agassiz, the rubberlip surfperch, has lips that are very thick, making the species quite recognizable. Reaching a size of 47 cm, it is the largest surfperch. Photo by Daniel W. Gotshall.

219. *Abudefduf troscheli* (Gill), the Panamic sergeant major. This male in full courtship colors is attempting to attract females to his territory. Note the cleared area just below him. Photo of a 9-cm male by Alex Kerstitch at Cabo San Lucas, Baja California, Mexico.

220. A normally colored *Abudefduf troscheli* of about the same size (9 cm). This species has a wide range, from Baja California to Peru and the Galapagos Islands. It has a geminate (twin) species in the Atlantic called *Abudefduf saxatilis,* and the two were once thought to be synonymous. Photo by Alex Kerstitch at Cabo San Lucas, Baja California, Mexico.

221. *Nexilarius concolor* (Gill) (or *Abudefduf declevifrons* or possibly *Nexilarius declevifrons,* if the species and genera are distinct) prefers the surf zone of rocky beaches from Baja California to Peru. **Photo by Dr. R. E.** Thresher at Cabo Pulmo, Gulf of California, Mexico.

222. *Abudefduf saxatilis* (Linnaeus), the sergeant major, is so much like *A. troscheli* (opposite) that many scientists consider them one and the same species. Photo by Dr. Walter A. Starck II of an individual from the Caribbean (Florida).

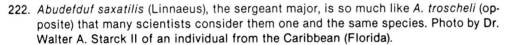

223. *Chromis atrilobata* Gill, the scissortail damselfish, is a common species extending from the Gulf of California to northern Peru and the Galapagos Islands. Photo by Alex Kerstitch of a subadult specimen 6.8 cm in length at 4.5 meters depth at Bahia San Carlos, Sonora, Mexico.

224. The scissortail damselfish may be seen in large aggregations such as this one. The characteristic white spot at the base of the soft dorsal fin is easily seen, especially in darker areas, and may be a recognition signal to keep the school together. Photo by Alex Kerstitch at 55 meters depth at Cabo San Lucas, Baja California, Mexico.

225. *Chromis punctipinnis* (Cooper), the blacksmith, is a more northerly species than *C. atrilobata,* occurring from central Baja California north to Monterey Bay. Photo by Daniel W. Gotshall at Catalina Island, California.

226. The blacksmith usually is found in the vicinity of rocks or kelp at depths to 46 meters. Breeding males **are** said to have a dark bar through the eye. Photo by Ken Lucas at Steinhart Aquarium.

227. *Chromis* sp. (undescribed species), the blue-and-yellow chromis, occurs at dephs of 18 to 76 meters in the Gulf of California. Photo by Alex Kerstitch of a juvenile about 2.5 cm in length at San Carlos, Sonora, Mexico.

228. Blue-and-yellow chromis adults about 10 cm in length. The dark spot is part of the background, not of the fish. Photo taken at a depth of about 25 meters by Alex Kerstitch at San Carlos, Sonora, Mexico.

229. *Chromis altus* Woods & Allen, the silverstripe chromis. Juveniles are iridescent blue and lack the white stripe of the adult. They resemble the juveniles of the Cortez damselfish. Photo by Alex Kerstitch of a juvenile about 5 cm in length collected at a depth of 23 meters at Isla San Pedro Martir, Sonora, Mexico.

230. An adult silverstripe chromis showing the characteristic stripe. This species is said to be more aggressive than the blue-and-yellow chromis. Photo by Alex Kerstitch of an individual 8.6 cm long at a depth of 75 meters in the Gulf of California.

231. *Pomacentrus redemptus* Heller & Snodgrass, the Clarion damselfish, has dark scale edges giving a mesh-like pattern to the darker part of the fish. This species is common in the Revillagigedo Islands and apparently has reached the mainland at Baja. Photo by Dr. R. E. Thresher at Cabo San Lucas, Baja California, Mexico.

232. The juvenile *Pomacentrus redemptus* is almost totally yellow with dark dorsal and upper peduncular spots. The darkening of the anterior body is starting to become obvious. Photo by Dr. R. E. Thresher at Cabo San Lucas, Baja California, Mexico. (Some authorities place this species in genus *Stegastes*).

233. *Pomacentrus rectifraenum* Gill, the Cortez damselfish, with the juvenile coloration (overall iridescent purplish blue). The juveniles are non-territorial and aggregate in shallow water over rocky substrates. Photo by Alex Kerstitch of an individual about 7.5 cm in length about 6 meters deep at Bahia San Carlos, Sonora, Mexico.

234. An adult *Pomacentrus rectifraenum* is chocolate brown to lighter brownish in color. It is territorial even to the extent of attacking much larger fishes than itself as well as curious skin divers. Photo by Alex Kerstitch of a 10-cm individual at Guaymas, Mexico. (Also placed by some in *Stegastes*.)

235. *Pomacentrus flavilatus* Gill, the beau brummel, has a juvenile that looks very much like the Caribbean beau gregory (*P. leucostictus*), but it may be more closely related to the similar appearing *P. variabilis* (also from the Caribbean). Photo by Alex Kerstitch of a 5-cm-long individual at Manzanillo, Colima, Mexico.

236. The less colorful adult beau brummel is also territorial. It feeds on benthic algae and small invertebrates. Photo by Alex Kerstitch of a 10-cm individual at a depth of 12 meters at Guaymas, Mexico. (This species is placed by some in *Stegastes*.)

237. *Pomacentrus leucorus* Gilbert, the whitetail damselfish, as a juvenile (seen here) has brighter colors than the adult. The adult is a dull bluish brown with a white band at the caudal base and pale margins to the dark pectoral fins. Photo by Alex Kerstitch of a 5-cm juvenile at Isla San Jose, Baja California, Mexico. (This species is placed by some in *Stegastes*.)

238. *Microspathodon bairdi* (Gill), the bumphead damselfish, does not have the trailing fin streamers of the giant damselfish but does have a more prominent bump on the nape. The juveniles are like those of the beau brummel, i.e., iridescent blue above the lateral line and yellowish orange below. Photo of an adult by Dr. R. E. Thresher at Cabo Pulmo, Gulf of California.

239. *Microspathodon dorsalis* (Gill), the giant damselfish, juveniles are bright blue like juvenile Cortez damselfish but differ in possessing the pale blue spots as seen in this photo. Photo by Alex Kerstitch of a subadult about 12.5 cm in length at Guaymas, Sonora, Mexico.

240. An adult *Microspathodon dorsalis* in breeding color (pale head, dark body). Non-breeding adults are overall blue (dark or light blue). Note also the prolongation of the unpaired fins. Photo by Alex Kerstitch of an individual about 26 cm in length at Cabo San Lucas, Baja California, Mexico, at a depth of 4-5 meters.

251. The male *Bodianus diplotaenia* is quite different, with a brownish gray body color and a bright yellow mid-body bar. Note that the fins are prolonged. This is the shallow-water form. Photo by Alex Kerstitch of a 30-cm individual at Cabo San Lucas, Baja California, Mexico.

252. An adult male Mexican hogfish (from deep water) with a predominantly reddish body. However, the yellow bar is still present. Note also the black tips of the pectoral fins. Photo by Alex Kerstitch of a 40-cm male at 80 meters depth at Sheppard's Rock, Cabo San Lucas, Baja California, Mexico.

253. In *Halichoeres dispilus* (Guenther), the chameleon wrasse, males can be colored quite differently from the females, the shoulder spot being one of the few color features they have in common. Over a different substrate they may turn reddish like the females, hence the common name chameleon wrasse. Photo by Dr. Gerald R. Allen of a 13-cm male from Panama.

254. The red phase or female of the chameleon wrasse. The shoulder spot, although of a different color, can still be seen. This species is one of those that sleeps under the sand at night or dives into the sand when frightened. Photo by Dr. Gerald R. Allen of a 10-cm individual from Panama.

255. *Halichoeres* sp. This specimen has many color pattern elements similar to those of the wounded wrasse below, but its identity is still uncertain. Photo of a 10-cm specimen from Panama by Dr. Gerald R. Allen.

256. *Halichoeres chierchiae* Caporiacco, the wounded wrasse, is so-called because of the blood-red color marking or "wound" below the dorsal fin of the adult male. This species can be seen over shallow reefy areas with patches of sand. Photo of an adult male by Dr. R. E. Thresher at Cabo Pulmo, Gulf of California, Mexico.

257. *Halichoeres nicholsi* (Jordan & Gilbert), the spinster wrasse, is difficult to maintain in aquaria because of its prolonged disappearing act beneath the sand. When it does emerge it is usually in bad shape, having not eaten while it was buried. Photo by Alex Kerstitch of an 18-cm female at 10 meters depth at San Carlos, Sonora, Mexico.

258. The male spinster wrasse is differently patterned, having a diffuse lateral blotch with a yellow streak immediately before it. Photo by Alex Kerstitch of a 30-cm adult male at 10 meters depth at Isla San Pedro Martir, Sonora, Mexico.

259. *Halichoeres nicholsi* juvenile of about 6 cm length. Photo by Alex Kerstitch of a specimen from San Agustin, Sonora, Mexico.

260. A slightly older specimen with the pattern starting to change. Photo by Dr. Gerald R. Allen of a specimen from Panama.

261. A still older spinster wrasse with more evident color pattern changes. Note the blackish bar starting to make its appearance. Photo by Dr. Gerald R. Allen of a 10-cm specimen from Panama.

262. *Pseudojulis melanotis* Gilbert, the golden wrasse, has a juvenile with a prominent dark band on a golden and whitish body color. Adults are similar but not as brightly colored. Photo by Alex Kerstitch of a 7.5-cm individual at a depth of 18 meters at Isla Blanca, Sonora, Mexico.

263. *Pseudojulis notospilus* Guenther, the banded wrasse, occurs from the Gulf of California to Peru and the Galapagos Islands. It feeds principally on crustaceans, molluscs, and even sea urchins. Photo by Alex Kerstitch of a 16.6-cm adult from a depth of 6 meters at San Carlos, Sonora, Mexico.

264. *Halichoeres semicinctus* (Ayres), the rock wrasse, stays close to rocks near sand patches where it can sleep at night or dive for safety. Photo by Daniel W. Gotshall, San Benitos.

265. The female rock wrasse lacks the blackish bar but has black flecks as in the juveniles. Females are said to change to males at a length of 30 cm. Photo by Daniel W. Gotshall, San Martin Island, Baja California, Mexico.

266. *Hemipteronotus pavoninus* (Valenciennes), the Pacific razorfish, is another Indo-Pacific species that has crossed the East Pacific Barrier to the tropical eastern Pacific. This frightened juvenile has pointed its elongate dorsal spine forward, a common reaction. Photo by Alex Kerstitch of a 7.5-cm individual from Cabo San Lucas, Baja California, Mexico.

The Cortez rainbow wrasse, *Thalassoma lucasanum*, is brightly colored and therefore easy to recognize. The supermales are purplish blue with a bright yellow shoulder band, while juveniles and other adults are striped with red and yellow. This species frequents rocky coasts in warmer waters (from which it may absent itself if the winter becomes too cool) in loose aggregations. By day they can be seen feeding on crustaceans, algae, and soft coral, whereas at night they retire to rock crevices where they are only partly covered by sand. In captivity they are said to be quite aggressive.

267. *Semicossyphus pulcher* (Ayres), the California sheepshead, juveniles differ from the adult fish in color pattern but are easily recognized by their white lateral stripe and black spots on the fins and caudal peduncle. Photo by Daniel W. Gotshall at Catalina Island, California.

268. An adult male *Semicossyphus pulcher* in its typical habitat of rocky bottoms around kelp beds. Photo by Daniel W. Gotshall at San Benito Island.

269. The female California sheepshead is more plainly colored, with a yellowish red body and white chin. Photo of a 25-cm female by Dr. Gerald R. Allen at Steinhart Aquarium.

270. Close-up of the head of a male California sheepshead at Steinhart Aquarium. Fully grown individuals can attain a length of about one meter. This fish is becoming rare because of fishing pressure. Photo by Dr. Herbert R. Axelrod.

271. *Oxyjulis californica* Guenther, the senorita, in its natural habitat. This species is often seen in small groups well off the bottom in kelp and over rocks. Photo by Daniel W. Gotshall at San Martin Island, Baja California, Mexico.

272. The senorita when threatened or frightened will dive into the sand. It is also said to sleep buried in the sand with only its head exposed. Photo by Ken Lucas at Steinhart Aquarium.

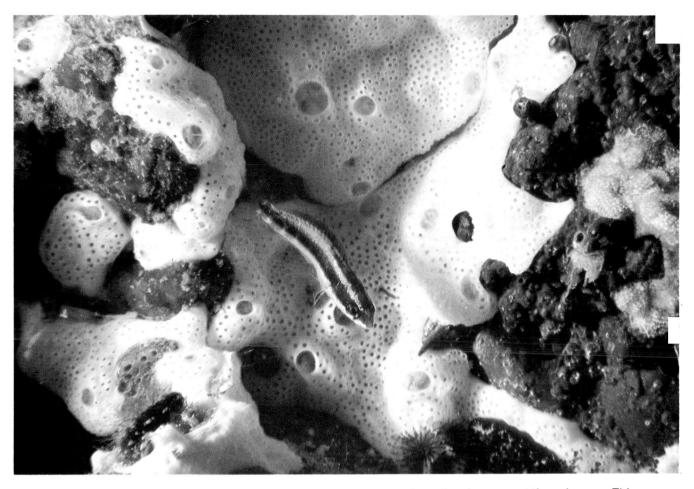

273. *Thalassoma lucasanum* (Gill), the Cortez rainbow wrasse, has juveniles that are part-time cleaners. This one is ready to retreat into the reef crevice at a moment's notice. Photo by Alex Kerstitch of a 2.5-cm individual in its typical habitat at Cabo San Lucas, Baja California, Mexico.

274. A partially grown Cortez rainbow wrasse possibly starting to change into a supermale's livery. Photo by Aaron Norman of a 7.5-cm individual.

275. A spawning aggregation of *Thalassoma lucasanum.* No supermales are seen here for they are not group spawners; they select individual females to spawn with. Photo by Alex Kerstitch at 10 meters depth at Isla Catalina, San Carlos, Mexico.

276. A supermale Cortez rainbow wrasse in full color. Supermales are always more brightly colored than the normal males and females of the species. Photo by Dr. Gerald R. Allen of a 15-cm male at Steinhart Aquarium.

277. Young parrotfishes are notoriously difficult to identify. This pair of specimens (top, 5. 4 cm; bottom, 3.8 cm) is probably *Nicholsina denticulata* (Evermann & Radcliffe), the loosetooth parrotfish. Photo by Alex Kerstitch of specimens from about 9 meters depth at Guaymas, Sonora, Mexico.

278. *Scarus perrico* Jordan & Gilbert, the bumphead parrotfish, is so-called because of the swelling at the nape so obvious in this photograph. Both sexes develop the bump at a large size. The male seen here is 60 cm in length; the female just above and behind him is about 30 cm (no bump yet). Photo by Alex Kerstitch at 12 meters depth at Guaymas, Sonora, Mexico.

Family OPISTOGNATHIDAE
JAWFISHES

Jawfishes are burrowing fishes with large heads and large mouths to match. Their eyes have an anterior notch like that found in the eyes of groupers. They are quite capable burrowers in bottoms that are sandy but supplied with many small stones or coral rubble. These small stones are used to surround the entrances to their burrows and are replaced if they are washed away or moved too far away to please the jawfish. In fact, this housekeeping is attended to so assiduously that when a jawfish is brooding eggs, the eggs are set down long enough for the burrow to be repaired and then carefully taken up again. With or without eggs, jawfishes actively guard the entrances to their burrows against almost all intruders. After threatening or chasing the intruder, the jawfish will usually return to its burrow tail-first. The family is said to contain approximately 40 species included in only three genera, of which about eight species are found in the eastern Pacific region (as many as five of these probably are still undescribed).

Spawning was observed in *Opistognathus rhomaleus*. The parent (later determined to be the female) carried a clutch of eggs for three to four days, during which time the eggs were rotated within the mouth. Spawning was repeated at intervals of 10 to 30 days for awhile, but none of the eggs hatched.

The blue-spotted jawfish (one of the undescribed forms) apparently is relatively common on the offshore islands near bases of rocky cliffs or outcroppings offshore, occurring in colonies of up to several hundred individuals. The normal and courtship color patterns are quite different and are well represented by the photos on the following pages.

279. An unidentified jawfish (*Opistognathus* sp.), possibly undescribed, that has been called the mottled jawfish. This one, of about 10 cm length, was photographed during a night dive by Alex Kerstitch at 12 meters at Punta Chivato, Baja California, Mexico.

280. *Opistognathus punctatus* Peters, the finespotted jawfish, has a capacious mouth typical of jawfishes. This is used, among other things, to construct a burrow in the substrate. Photo by Alex Kerstitch of a specimen trawled at a depth of 90 meters at Morro Colorado, Sonora, Mexico.

281. *Opistognathus rhomaleus* Jordan & Gilbert, the giant jawfish, attains a length of over 50 cm. It's distinguished from *O. punctatus* by the smaller body spotting. Photo by Ken Lucas at Steinhart Aquarium.

282. *Opistognathus* sp., the blue-spotted jawfish, is as yet undescribed. This is a male in his breeding coloration, a bicolored pattern very different from the normal pattern shown on the opposite page. Photo by Alex
Kerstitch at Isla San Pedro Martir, Sonora, Mexico.

283. Blue-spotted jawfish males remain motionless for two to three seconds 30-60 cm above their burrows. They
will then suddenly dart into the burrows. Photo by Alex Kerstitch at Isla San Pedro Martir, Sonora, Mexico.

284. A blue-spotted jawfish in its normal coloration, showing the blue spots that give rise to its common name. Photo by Alex Kerstitch of an individual about 12.5 cm in length at Isla San Pedro Nolasco, Sonora, Mexico.

285. A close-up of the head of the blue-spotted jawfish. Note the "grouper eye" with the anterior edge drawn out for better binocular vision. Photo by Alex Kerstitch at Isla San Pedro Nolasco, Sonora, Mexico.

286. *Opistognathus scops* (Jenkins & Evermann), the bull's-eye jawfish, showing typical threat behavior. The large ocellated spot of course gave rise to the common name. Photo by Alex Kerstitch.

287. A probable new species of *Opistognathus.* This individual, about 8 cm in length, is just poking its head out of its burrow. Photo by Alex Kerstitch of an individual from Guaymas, Sonora, Mexico.

Family BATHYMASTERIDAE
RONQUILS

The Bathymasteridae is a small family of a half dozen or more species distributed in the North Pacific. Most are smallish, with the largest species attaining a length of no more than 30 cm. They are moderately elongate, with long dorsal and anal fins. Both these fins are composed of only rays (no spines), the number of unbranched rays in the dorsal fin being of great significance in determining the identity of the genera.

Not much is known about the life history of these fishes. The northern ronquil, *Ronquilus jordani*, is perhaps best known. It inhabits depths of about 14 to 165 meters from Monterey Bay in California to the Bering Sea. According to observations made on aquarium-housed individuals, spawning takes place after a lengthy courtship. Since females captured in March have contained fully developed amber or salmon-colored eggs, spawning itself must occur around that time or shortly thereafter. The northern ron-

quil produces what has been described as a loose, flat egg mass. Young fish between 5 and 11 mm in length were found to be feeding on various crustaceans such as copepods and barnacle larvae, clam larvae, and polychaete worms.

Another species, the smooth ronquil (*Rathbunella hypoplecta*), inhabits rocky coastal areas of California and Baja California at depths of from 10 to 100 meters. Apparent sexual dimorphism occurs in which the tips of the anal rays are black in the male while those of the females are white. According to aquarium observations, a female spawned at two-week intervals for a total of six times, laying approximately 10,000 eggs per spawn in a secluded area. The spawnings occurred within a day or so of the time the current spawn hatched, and the male remained on guard for the duration of the incubation period, although he sometimes ate some of the eggs he was guarding.

Ronquils eat a variety of invertebrates. Crustaceans are preferred, but nudibranchs were found in the stomachs of some individuals.

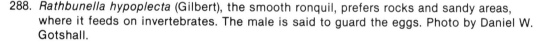

288. *Rathbunella hypoplecta* (Gilbert), the smooth ronquil, prefers rocks and sandy areas, where it feeds on invertebrates. The male is said to guard the eggs. Photo by Daniel W. Gotshall.

Family DACTYLOSCOPIDAE
SAND STARGAZERS

The sand stargazers are few in number, perhaps only two dozen species, and are distributed mainly in tropical marine waters of the New World. Several species may enter brackish waters of estuaries, and at least one species in the eastern Pacific enters fresh water. Sand stargazers are often confused with the electric stargazers of the family Uranoscopidae but differ from that family by lacking the electric organs and having three instead of five rays in the ventral fins. In addition, sand stargazers have a well developed lateral line, something that is absent in the electric stargazers. They are generally small, sand-dwelling forms, often with stalked eyes, and the lips are usually fringed.

The habit of burying themselves in the sand is highly developed and is accomplished by movements of the large pectoral fins and wriggling movements of the body and anal fin. When fully buried, often only the eyes are visible; at other times the head and part of the back are exposed, but a buried sand stargazer is still almost impossible to detect, for its coloration blends in with the sand almost perfectly. The ability to take in water for breathing without a great deal of sand as well is accomplished with the help of the fringed lips that act as sort of a sieve.

Some species (at least one species in each of the three genera *Dactyloscopus*, *Dactylagnus*, and *Myxodagnus*) have been observed to incubate their eggs in a most unusual way: the eggs are carried in two rounded masses, one under each pectoral fin. It was discovered that in at least one of the species the incubating parent was the male, but in the other species the sex of the parent has yet to be determined.

Family URANOSCOPIDAE
ELECTRIC STARGAZERS

The family Uranoscopidae is a small family of about two dozen species distributed in tropical and temperate marine waters of the world both in shallow and very deep waters. In appearance they are very much like the Dactyloscopidae and can be distinguished

289. *Dactyloscopus pectoralis* Gill, the red-saddled sand stargazer, is commonly encountered in sandy areas of rocky tide pools. Photo of a 7.5-cm individual taken by Alex Kerstitch during a night dive at a depth of 12 meters at Punta Chivato, Baja California, Mexico.

290. *Kathetostoma averruncus* Jordan & Bollman, the smooth stargazer, in a head-on view. It usually remains buried (or partially buried) in the bottom waiting for potential prey to pass by. Note the fringe-like papillae on the lips. Photo by Alex Kerstitch.

from that family by the characters mentioned in the preceding discussion. The electric stargazers are also burrowers in the sand and are usually found with only the tops of their heads visible. The eyes are placed in such a way so that they are directed upward when the fish is buried, hence the common name "stargazers." In some species the nostril opens directly into the mouth, allowing the passage of water without the problem of sediment or sand grains clogging the gills. In certain species there is a small "fishing lure" shaped like a worm attached to the mouth to entice prey fishes to the vicinity of the cavernous mouth.

The electric stargazers, as the common name implies, have electric organs that can produce electrical shocks of up to 50 volts. The electric organs are found in special pouches behind the eyes and are said to be derived from optic nerve tissue. As if this were not enough, some electric stargazers are provided with two poisonous spines above each pectoral fin just behind the opercles. Each spine is grooved, and the spines are surrounded by venom glands. In some species the venom from these glands is extremely toxic; human deaths have been recorded as the result of stings by these fishes.

Families BLENNIIDAE, CLINIDAE, TRIPTERYGIIDAE, and CHAENOPSIDAE
BLENNIES

Although there are a number of other blennoid families, the four covered here are those most commonly seen and contain the fishes most usually thought of when the name blenny is used. The Blenniidae proper are the combtooth blennies; the Clinidae are the clinid blennies; the Tripterygiidae are the triplefin blennies; and the Chaenopsidae are the tube blennies or pikeblennies.

The tube blennies or pikeblennies are small, elongate fishes that are scaleless and have at most a vestigial lateral line. The dorsal fin is complete (unnotched), with twice as many spines as soft rays, and there are well developed head cirri. Some workers combine the chaenopsids with the clinids, but current thought is that they represent separate families. The approximately 11 genera with 40 or so species inhabit tropical to subtropical regions, primarily of the Western Hemisphere. The tube blennies are so-called because they commonly take up residence in abandoned tubes of various invertebrates (such as tubeworms). The male engages in elaborate courtship maneuvers involving his large dorsal fin and movements in and out of the tube in rapid succession. Females thus attracted will deposit their eggs in the tube, where the male guards them.

The clinid blennies (including the kelpfishes and fringeheads) are also small, elongate fishes, but they have well developed cycloid scales and conical teeth (triplefins have ctenoid scales, and the blenniids and chaenopsids lack scales). The dorsal fin is long, usually with more spines than soft rays,

291. *Acanthemblemaria crockeri* Beebe & Tee-Van, the browncheek blenny, usually inhabits abandoned worm tubes or other invertebrate burrows in rocky areas. Photo by Alex Kerstitch of a female about 4.5 cm in length at Guaymas, Sonora, Mexico.

292. *Acanthemblemaria crockeri* males are more uniformly colored than the females and have numerous light dots covering the body. Photo by Alex Kerstitch of a specimen about 4.9 cm long collected at a depth of 4.5 meters at Guaymas, Sonora, Mexico.

293. The female browncheek blenny has a barred pattern on her body. Note the large brownish cheek spot in both sexes (it is present in juveniles as well). Photo by Dr. M. Brittan.

294. *Acanthemblemaria macrospilus* Brock, the clubhead blenny, is similar to *A. crockeri* but has a crimson area in the anterior portion of the dorsal fin. Photo by Alex Kerstitch of a male about 5 cm long taken at La Paz, Baja California, Mexico.

295. *Acanthemblemaria balanorum* Brock, the barnacle blenny, ranges from Baja California to Panama. The type of head spines, the color of the head, and the body pattern help distinguish this species from others in the area. Photo by Alex Kerstitch of a male about 5 cm long from Cabo San Lucas, Baja California, Mexico.

296. *Acanthemblemaria hancocki* Myers & Reid, Hancock's blenny. This is a female about 4 cm long. Note the absence of the orange in the first rays of the dorsal fin. Photo by Dr. Gerald R. Allen of a specimen from Panama.

297. *Acanthemblemaria hancocki* Myers & Reid, a male of about the same size (4 cm) with the characteristic dorsal fin coloration as well as the orange spot at the pectoral fin base. Photo by Dr. Gerald R. Allen of a specimen from Panama.

298. *Acanthemblemaria exilispinis* Stephans, the slender-spined blenny, has a well-developed supraorbital cirrus. Photo of a 4 cm specimen taken by Dr. Gerald R. Allen at Perlas Archipelago, Panama.

299. *Coralliozetus springeri* Stephens & Johnson, Springer's blenny, is found toward the southern end of our range, from Panama to Ecuador. Photo by Dr. Gerald R. Allen of a specimen from Panama.

300. *Neoclinus blanchardi* Girard, the sarcastic fringehead, has two ocellated spots in the dorsal fin (seen in this photo). They are blue with a gold ring surrounding them. Photo by Daniel W. Gotshall at Santo Tomas, Baja California, Mexico.

301. *Coralliozetus angelica* (Boehlke & Mead), the angel blenny, has a very distinctive male nuptial coloration as seen here. The orange face and throat contrast with the brown head and yellow orbital cirri. Photo by Alex Kerstitch of a 3.5-cm male from Isla San Pedro Martir, Sonora, Mexico.

302. *Coralliozetus micropes* (Beebe & Tee-Van), the scarletfin blenny, occupies various refuges including such things as worm and mollusc tubes and barnacle tests. Photo by Alex Kerstitch of a 2.5-3-cm individual at 1.5 meters depth at Isla Blanca, Sonora, Mexico.

303. *Ekemblemaria myersi* Stephens, the reefsand blenny, has a cheek spot and a single pair of beige branched orbital cirri. Note the very dark dorsal and anal fins with the light trim. Photo by Dr. Gerald R. Allen of a 5-cm specimen from Panama.

304. The reefsand blenny has a range from the Gulf of California to Ecuador and prefers rocky areas surrounded by sandy bottom. Photo by Dr. Gerald R. Allen of a 3.5-cm specimen from Panama.

305. *Chaenopsis alepidota* (Gilbert), the orangethroat pikeblenny, occupies invertebrate tubes like many of the other species. Here an individual is entering a tube tail-first. Photo by Alex Kerstitch of a 10-cm individual at 6 meters depth at Morro Colorado, Sonora, Mexico.

306. An orangethroat pikeblenny in its threat posture with the mouth wide open and body curled. Males are territorial, defending their tubes from interlopers. Photo of an 8-cm male by Aaron Norman.

307. *Emblemaria walkeri* Stephens, the elusive blenny, is a rare blenny known only from the Gulf of California. Photo by Alex Kerstitch of a male about 6 cm long from La Paz, Baja California, Mexico.

308. *Emblemaria walkeri* females are less colorful and have a much less elevated anterior part of the dorsal fin. Photo by Alex Kerstitch of a 5-cm female from Isla San Pedro Nolasco, Sonora, Mexico.

309. *Emblemaria hypacanthus* (Jenkins & Evermann), the signal blenny, will accept a variety of tubes for its home and will defend its territory against all intruders. The raising of the sail-like dorsal fin is both a signal to warn off trespassers and a courtship display, this latter accompanied by a darkening of the colors as seen here. Photo of Guaymas, Mexico, specimens by Alex Kerstitch.

310. *Protemblemaria bicirris* (Hildebrand), the warthead blenny, has a fairly limited range, occurring in the Gulf of California and on the Pacific coast of Baja California to Bahia Magdalena. Photo by Alex Kerstitch of a male about 3 cm long at Guaymas, Sonora, Mexico.

311. *Protemblemaria lucasana* Stephens, the plume blenny, is not seen very often in an exposed condition such as this individual. This species is endemic to the Gulf of California. Photo by Alex Kerstitch of a male about 4.6 cm long from Isla San Pedro Martir, Sonora, Mexico.

312. The plume blenny in its worm tube residence. The plume-like orbital cirri that gave rise to its common name can plainly be seen. Photo by Alex Kerstitch of an individual from Isla San Pedro Nolasco, Sonora, Mexico.

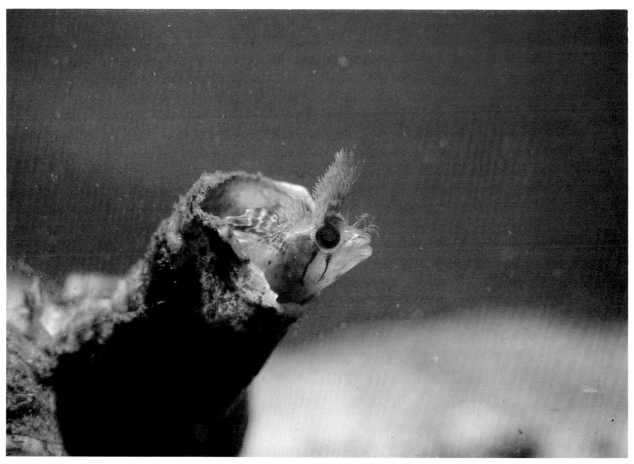

313. *Exerpes asper* (Jenkins & Evermann), the sargassum blenny, is closely associated with *Sargassum* and *Zostera* (eelgrass) and may be found within its range wherever they are abundant. Photo by Alex Kerstitch of an adult about 5 cm in length from Guaymas, Sonora, Mexico.

314. A somewhat smaller sargassum blenny. Juveniles stay in small schools but become more antisocial with growth. They also depend upon camouflage for protection more so than flight and are easy to catch once seen. Photo by Alex Kerstitch of a 3-cm individual from Puerto Pennasco, Sonora, Mexico.

315. *Stathmonotus sinuscalifornici* (Chabanaud), the worm blenny, lacks scales, has a lateral line, and occurs from Puerto Lobos, Sonora, to Cabo San Lucas. It is rarely seen. Photo of an adult 7.5 cm in length in winter coloration from Guaymas, Sonora, Mexico, by Alex Kerstitch.

316. *Malacoctenus tetranemus* (Cope), the throatspotted blenny, was first discovered at Pacasmayo Bay, Peru, and rediscovered at Lobos de Afuera Island, Peru. This 5-cm specimen was collected and photographed by Dr. Gerald R. Allen in Panama.

317. **Malacoctenus ebisui** Springer, the fishgod blenny, has a range from the Gulf of California (rare) to Panama. Photo of a 5-cm specimen from Panama by Dr. Gerald R. Allen.

318. *Malacoctenus* sp. (possibly *M. margaritae*) of about 3.8 cm from Panama. Photo by Dr. Gerald R. Allen.

319. **Malacoctenus zonifer sudensis** Springer, the girdled blenny, from the Pacific side of Panama. This 5-cm specimen was collected and photographed by Dr. Gerald R. Allen.

320. *Malacoctenus gigas* Springer, the Sonora blenny, is a relatively common blenny endemic to the Gulf of California. Principal items in its diet are small crustaceans such as amphipods. Photo of a juvenile by Dr. R. E. Thresher at Bahia de Los Angeles, Gulf of California.

321. *Malacoctenus margaritae* (Fowler), the margarita blenny, is a more widely ranging species occurring from the Gulf of California to Panama. Photo of an adult about 5 cm long by Alex Kerstitch at a depth of 3 meters at San Agustin, Sonora, Mexico.

322. ? *Malacoctenus tetranemus* (Cope), the throatspotted blenny, is so called because of the profusion of black spots on the head and throat. Photo of an individual about 5 cm long by Alex Kerstitch at Guaymas, Sonora, Mexico.

323. *Alloclinus holderi* (Lauderbach), the island kelpfish, prefers rocky areas as shown. Photo by Daniel W. Gotshall at 10 meters depth at Little Harbor, Catalina, California.

324. *Paraclinus mexicanus* (Gilbert), the Mexican blenny, has a wide range, occurring from the Gulf of California to Ecuador. Specimens preserved in formalin turn black. Photo of a 4-cm individual by Alex Kerstitch at Guaymas, Sonora, Mexico.

325. The Mexican blenny lacks the flap-like projections on its scales that are found in its relatives. A dorsal ocellus also occurs in other species, so this is of limited help in identification. Photo by Dr. Gerald R. Allen of a 3.8-cm specimen from Panama.

326. *Starksia spinipenis* (Al-Uthman), the phallic blenny, has a relatively distinctive color pattern. It is common in the Gulf of California and extends south along the coast to Acapulco. Photo by Alex Kerstitch.

327. *Xenomedia rhodopyga* Rosenblatt & Taylor, the redrump blenny, is a livebearing blenny (as are all the closely related clinids) that inhabits rocky bottoms where there is sufficient algal growth. Photo by Alex Kerstitch.

328. *Labrisomus xanti* Gill, the largemouth blenny, is strongly territorial and feeds mainly on benthic crustaceans. Note the row of cirri crossing the nape (nuchal cirri). Photo of an individual about 15 cm long by Alex Kerstitch at a depth of 4.5 meters at Bahia San Carlos, Sonora, Mexico.

and all the fins have unbranched rays. Although most are less than 7.5 cm in length, *Labrisomus xanti* can reach more than twice that (about 18 cm). Most clinids are temperate to tropical inshore species that are cryptically colored and stay close to some shelter. Some species are livebearers, whereas others are typical egglayers. Almost all are bottom-dwellers, although at least one species, *Exerpes asper*, is closely associated with floating sargassum weed. The family contains an estimated 135 species relegated to about 30 genera.

The triplefin blennies (Tripterygiidae) are so-called because the dorsal fin is divided into three distinct sections, the first two composed of spines, the last including soft rays. They are scaled blennies with ctenoid scales (clinids have cycloid scales). Most species are small, less than 7.5 cm long, and inhabit intertidal waters where they can be seen on the rock surfaces.

The combtooth blennies (Blenniidae) have, as the name implies, teeth that are arranged in close-set rows like that of a comb. They are small, scaleless, with steep, blunt heads provided with big, high-set eyes and prominent fleshy cirri. The dorsal fin is long, usually without a notch, and with approximately equal numbers of flexible spines and soft rays. Combtooth blennies are common intertidally in rocky zones of tropical and subtropical (some temperate) waters worldwide. Many are grazers that also feed on sessile invertebrates, although it is said that they are voracious carnivores in captivity. About 275 species are included in some 46 genera.

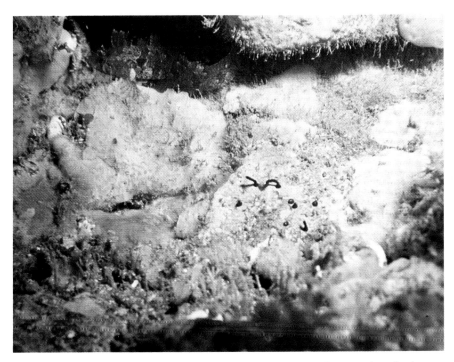

329. *Gibbonsia montereyensis* Hubbs, the crevice kelpfish, prefers inshore
rocky areas where there is sufficient algae. Its range extends from British
Columbia to northern Baja California. Photo by Daniel W. Gotshall.

330. *Gibbonsia metzi* Hubbs, the striped kelpfish, may be seen in tidepools among seaweeds and
kelp. Photo by Ken Lucas at Steinhart Aquarium.

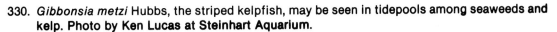

331. *Heterostichus rostratus* Girard, the giant kelpfish, is the only kelpfish with a forked caudal fin. It grows quite large, attaining a length of over 60 cm. Photo by Daniel W. Gotshall.

332. *Enneanectes sexmaculatus* (Fowler), the delicate triplefin, is a small, delicate-appearing species ranging from the Gulf of California to Panama. Photo by Dr. Gerald R. Allen of a specimen about maximum size for the species (2.5 cm) from Panama.

333. The lizard triplefin is an as yet undescribed genus and species. It is endemic to the Gulf of California, where it occurs on rocky coasts from intertidal waters to depths of greater than 30 meters. Photo by Alex Kerstitch of a 6.1-cm specimen from Guaymas, Sonora, Mexico.

334. The lizard triplefin in its natural habitat. It is said that individuals often perch on boulders in shallow water, slowly waving the flag-like tail back and forth. Photo by Alex Kerstitch of an individual about 7.5 cm long at Isla San Pedro Nolasco, Sonora, Mexico.

335. Another undescribed species of triplefin. This one, about 3.8 cm in length, was collected and photographed by Dr. Gerald R. Allen in Panama.

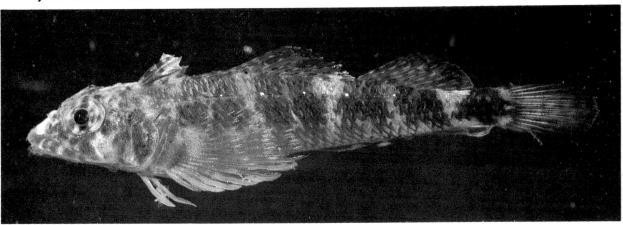

336. *Hypsoblennius brevipinnis* (Guenther), the barnaclebill blenny, received its common name due to its inclination of living in empty barnacle tests. Photo by Dr. Gerald R. Allen of a 13-cm specimen from Panama.

337. *Hypsoblennius gentilis* (Girard), the bay blenny, is another highly territorial blenny. It is a hardy species that will adapt well to captivity and has even spawned in aquaria. Photo of a 7.5-cm individual by Alex Kerstitch at Guaymas, Sonora, Mexico.

338. *Ophioblennius steindachneri* Jordan & Evermann, the Panamic fanged blenny, is so-called because of a pair of large canine teeth in the rear of the lower jaw. It has a close Atlantic relative (geminate species), *O. atlanticus*. Photo by Dr. Gerald R. Allen of a 12.5 cm specimen from Panama.

339. A Panamic fanged blenny specimen of a smaller size (5 cm). The pelagic larvae of this blenny are said to have anterior fangs that disappear at metamorphosis. Photo of a specimen from Panama by Dr. Gerald R. Allen.

340. *Plagiotremus azaleus* (Jordan & Bollman), the sabertooth blenny, like its Indo-Pacific cousins mimics other fishes (in this case *Thalassoma lucasanum*) to approach them and then feeds on their skin mucus. Photo of a 7.5-cm specimen from Panama by Dr. Gerald R. Allen.

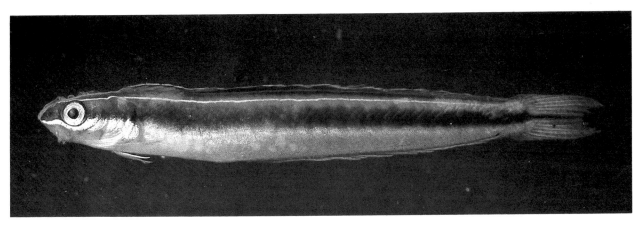

Family STICHAEIDAE
PRICKLEBACKS

The more than 50 species of this family are elongate to moderately elongate bottom-dwelling fishes that are circumboreal in distribution. They have a long-based dorsal fin composed entirely or almost entirely of spines (a few species may have some soft rays posteriorly); the dorsal fin may or may not be confluent with the caudal fin. The anal fin is long and sometimes confluent with the caudal fin, while the pelvic fins are composed of a spine and three to four rays or may be absent entirely. The teeth of the jaws are small and conical.

Included within this family are fishes with common names such as pricklebacks, cockscombs, warbonnets, and the well-known shanny. Information on life histories is available for some of the species. The high cockscomb, *Anoplarchus purpurescens*, for example, matures after two or three years, with the females growing a bit faster and therefore reaching a larger size than the males. Females also seem to be more numerous than males. The eggs, roughly 1.4 mm in diameter and more than 2500 in number, are deposited in a sheltered spot under rocks or shells where they are guarded by the female. She wraps her body around the egg mass, fanning them with undulating movements of the posterior portion of her body. In less than three weeks a 7.5 mm larva hatches out complete with yolk sac and still with an oil globule that was evident in the egg. On a diet composed almost exclusively of copepods, the young grow quickly and at a size of 2.5 cm or a little more they are miniature adults, cockscomb and all. As they grow, the diet expands to include such things as polychaetes and other worms, other crustaceans, molluscs, and green algae, the algae constituting approximately 32% of their food.

341. *Chirolophis nugator* (Jordan & Williams), the mosshead warbonnet, is easily recognized by the 12 ocelli or short bars on the dorsal fin. It ranges from the Aleutian Islands to southern California, inhabiting rocky subtidal areas to depths of about 80 meters. Photo by Daniel W. Gotshall at Diablo Canyon, California.

342. *Chirolophis decoratus* (Jordan & Snyder), the decorated warbonnet, has a large number of spines and cirri on its head. It grows to a length of about 42 cm. Photo of a 13-cm individual by Dr. Gerald R. Allen at Steinhart Aquarium.

343. A side view of the decorated warbonnet showing the head decorations from a different angle. The anemones surrounding the fish's hole are *Corynactis californica.* Photo by Ken Lucas at Steinhart Aquarium.

344. *Cebidichthys violaceus* (Girard), the monkeyface prickleback, is one of the more unusual fishes of the eastern Pacific. It is even placed in its own family, the Cebidichthyidae, by some workers. Photo by Dr. Herbert R. Axelrod at Steinhart Aquarium.

345. A closer view of the lumpy head of the monkeyface prickleback. This species is common in shallow rocky areas, including tide pools. Photo by Ken Lucas at Steinhart Aquarium.

Family ANARHICHADIDAE
WOLFFISHES

The wolffishes are moderate to large fishes (a couple of species attaining lengths of between 2 and 3 meters) that are normally placed in the same suborder as the blennies. There are about nine species, all Northern Hemisphere inhabitants, but only a couple occur in the eastern Pacific. All species are elongate; the typical wolffishes (*Anarhichas*) have a shorter body (about 85 vertebrae) when compared to *Anarrhichthys*, the wolf-eel (about 350 vertebrae). The dorsal fin is totally spinous, quite long, and confluent or nearly so with the caudal fin; the pelvic fins are completely absent. The teeth in the jaws are distinctive, being a combination of large canine (dog-like) teeth in the front of the jaws and massive grinding molariform teeth in the back of the jaws. Similar teeth are also present in the roof of the mouth. The scales are generally small, dispersed, and hidden deep in the skin.

Wolffishes and wolf-eels are essentially bottom-living fishes of deeper waters that feed primarily on benthic invertebrates, although fish remains are not unknown in their stomach contents. In captivity some do well on crustaceans, clams, mussels, sea urchins, and other hard-shelled invertebrates. In all species spawning takes place in the winter, the very large eggs (a little over 6 mm) being laid in clumps on the bottom. A female wolf-eel, *Anarrhichthys ocellatus*, was taken with her egg mass to the Vancouver Aquarium, where she remained protectively coiled around them. She did not eat until the young hatched out. Spawning by this same species was witnessed at the Tacoma Aquarium, but no details are available.

346. *Anarrhichthys ocellatus* Ayres, the wolf-eel, has a northern distribution, extending from the Sea of Japan and along the coast of Alaska to southern California. The depth range is from subtidal areas to more than 200 meters. Photo by Ken Lucas at Steinhart Aquarium.

347. The wolf-eel dines on hard-shelled invertebrates as well as fishes. It grows to over 20 cm, and the larger individuals are said to sometimes inflict painful bites on unwary people. Photo by Ken Lucas at Steinhart Aquarium.

348. *Anarrhichthys ocellatus* lays its eggs in rocky areas, where they are guarded by both the male and female. Young are orange anteriorly, and the spotting may merge into stripes in the posterior part of the body. Photo by Dr. Gerald R. Allen at Steinhart Aquarium.

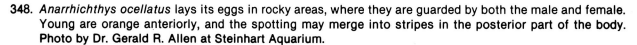

Family GOBIIDAE
GOBIES

The family Gobiidae is one of the most speciose groups of fishes in the world, with an estimated 2,000 species. As might be expected, there is great diversity in form and habit, with species found from tidal pools to deep water. Gobies are mostly tropical in distribution, although many extend into temperate regions as well. Most are marine fishes, but some species inhabit brackish water or even freshwater, and many have quite broad salinity tolerances. The majority of the gobies are bottom-dwellers. Some are burrowers—certain species are well-known for their symbiotic relationship with burrowing shrimp in which the shrimp builds the burrow and shrimp and fish live peacefully side-by-side—and there are even free-swimming midwater species. In general, gobies are small fishes, with the family including the smallest living vertebrates among their numbers. Several goby species have taken up the job (at least on a part-time basis) of cleaning other fishes.

Gobies are generally recognizable by the distinctive "goby" appearance combined with the united ventral fins forming a sort of sucking disc in almost all species. Some species are scaled, some are not. Most possess two separate dorsal fins, the first commonly composed of four to seven spines. The lateral line is usually absent on the sides of the body, but sensory lines and pores may be strongly developed on the head and jaws.

Perhaps the most well-known goby from the East Pacific is the Catalina goby, *Lythrypnus dalli*. Once thought rare, this spectacularly colored goby was discovered with the advent of SCUBA diving to be relatively common. Aquarists have found the species to be territorial, very aggressive, and, unfortunately, short-lived. Spawning has been observed, the male chasing the female accompanied by occasional nipping and nudging in an attempt to persuade her to accompany him to his territory. Once deposited, the eggs are guarded by the male until they hatch.

349. *Aruma histrio* (Jordan), the slow goby, is normally found in shallow areas and tide pools hiding under rocks or in deep crevices. Photo by Alex Kerstitch of an individual about 5 cm long from San Carlos, Sonora, Mexico.

350. *Chriolepis zebra* Ginsburg, the gecko goby, is a secretive species that is only rarely seen. It prefers rubble areas with many hiding places and white coralline sand in between. Photo by Dr. R. E. Thresher of an individual from Cabo Pulmo, Baja California, Mexico.

351. *Gobiosoma digueti* (Pellegrin), the banded cleaner goby, occurs in rocky areas to which larger fishes come to get rid of their parasites. Divers find that the goby will attempt to "clean" them as well. Photo by Alex Kerstitch of an individual about 3 cm long from Guaymas, Sonora, Mexico.

352. *Gobiosoma limbaughi* Hoese, the widebanded cleaning goby, is found with *G. digueti* but normally at greater depths. The bands of *G. limbaughi* are more regular. Photo by Alex Kerstitch of a 3-cm individual from Isla San Pedro Nolasco, Sonora, Mexico.

353. *Gobiosoma limbaughi* with even broader dark bands. The significance of the different color variations is as yet unknown. Photo by Alex Kerstitch of an individual about 3 cm long at a depth of 6 meters at Isla Blanca, Sonora, Mexico.

354. *Gobiosoma puncticulatus* Ginsburg, the redhead goby, has a wide range, occurring from the Gulf of California to Ecuador. The color pattern is distinctive. Photo by Dr. R. E. Thresher.

355. A top view of the redhead goby in its natural habitat. This shallow-water species is commonly found associated with *Eucidaris thouarsii,* the club-spined sea urchin. Photo by Alex Kerstitch of a 2.5-cm individual at a depth of 6 meters at Cabo San Lucas, Baja California, Mexico.

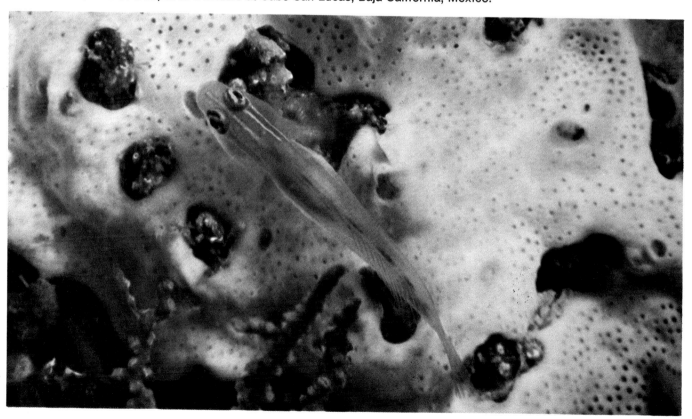

356. The redhead goby is an aggressive species and territorial. Actual battles are fought, including such maneuvers as jaw wrestling like that seen in the family Cichlidae. Photo of a 2.5-cm specimen from Panama by Dr. Gerald R. Allen.

357. *Gobiosoma* sp. This very pretty species was collected and photographed by Dr. Gerald R. Allen in Panama. It is about 2.5 cm in length.

358. *Gobiosoma chiquita* (Jenkins & Evermann), the Sonora goby, is a common species in intertidal rock pools with sandy bottoms. It feeds on small invertebrates, principally crustaceans. Photo by Dr. R. E. Thresher at La Paz, Gulf of California, Mexico.

359. *Lythrypnus pulchellus* Ginsburg, the gorgeous goby, is very similar to the bluebanded goby but has more blue bands than that species. Photo of a 2.5-cm individual by Alex Kerstitch at Isla San Pedro Nolasco, Sonora, Mexico.

360. *Lythrypnus dalli* (Gilbert), the bluebanded goby, is a short-lived goby, with few individuals lasting to the second year. Its very colorful pattern still makes it one of the most sought after eastern Pacific species. Photo by Ken Lucas at Steinhart Aquarium.

361. The bluebanded goby has a limited range, occurring from Morro Bay, California, to the Gulf of California. It prefers cooler water, occurring at depths of 50 meters and more in the summer but spread out through the depth range in the cooler winter months. Photo by Ken Lucas at Steinhart Aquarium.

362. *Coryphopterus nicholsi* (Bean), the blackeye goby, is usually seen in sandy areas among rocks but quickly disappears into the rocks when approached. Photo of a 15-cm individual by Dr. Gerald R. Allen at the Steinhart Aquarium.

363. A blackeye goby in its natural habitat. Spawning occurs under a rock, with the male guarding the eggs afterward. Photo by Daniel W. Gotshall.

364. Distinguishing characters of the blackeye goby are the black eye and the black tip of the first dorsal fin. The pelvic disc is black as well. Photo by Ken Lucas at Steinhart Aquarium.

365. *Coryphopterus urospilus* Ginsburg, the orangespot goby, in its natural habitat of rubble or rocky areas with sandy patches. It apparently forages over the sand for the major items of its diet, small crustaceans. Photo by Dr. Gerald R. Allen of a 3-cm individual at Panama.

366. A clinical shot of the orangespot goby. The orange spotting and the dark spot near the lower base of the caudal are recognition characters. Photo by Dr. Gerald R. Allen of a 5-cm specimen from Panama.

367. *Coryphopterus urospilus* in natural surroundings at Los Frailes, in the Gulf of California. Note the bright white dash below the eye and the row of white spots along the mid-dorsal line not seen in preserved specimens. Photo by Dr. R. E. Thresher.

368. *Ioglossus* sp., the Cortez hovering goby, is apparently an undescribed species from the Gulf of California. There may be one or two additional species of *Ioglossus* that are new to science in this region. Photo by Alex Kerstitch of a specimen about 10 cm long from 15 meters depth at Isla Blanca, Sonora, Mexico.

369. The Cortez hovering goby is so-called because of its habit of hovering a few centimeters above its burrow, feeding on the plankton that comes drifting by. Photo by Alex Kerstitch of individuals about 10 cm long at 30 meters depth at Guaymas, Sonora, Mexico.

Family ACANTHURIDAE
SURGEONFISHES

The surgeonfishes are distributed only in the warmer waters of our area of coverage. Worldwide the family comprises only about six or seven genera (depending upon whether or not *Zanclus*, the Moorish idol, is included or is placed in its own family) and about 75 to 80 species. In the eastern Pacific there are only a few species represented, most of them typical Indo-Pacific species such as *Acanthurus triostegus*, *A. achilles*, *A. glaucopareius*, *A. xanthopterus*, and *Zanclus canescens*. *Prionurus punctatus* is found only in the eastern Pacific.

The surgeonfishes are usually compressed, relatively deep-bodied fishes with characteristic sharp "scalpels" on each side of the caudal peduncle (except for *Zanclus*). These blades may be single and movable or multiple and fixed, but in all cases they are potentially dangerous weapons capable of inflicting painful wounds on human as well as fish enemies. An additional danger involved with surgeonfishes is the possibility of ciguatera poisoning if the flesh of certain species is eaten. Surgeonfishes are efficient algae scrapers and can often be seen in large schools grazing on rock and coral surfaces. This diet is often difficult to supply or to provide a substitute for in order to feed surgeonfishes kept in captivity, and for that reason many of the species are very difficult to maintain.

The yellowtail surgeonfish, *Prionurus punctatus*, has three fixed caudal peduncle spines. Its body is covered with black spots over a grayish background, although juveniles have a second and quite different color pattern. This alternate pattern is a bright overall yellow (this is not unique in the family, as several species have yellow juveniles). A yellow juvenile was seen to change to the normal spotted color pattern after a week in captivity. This species can commonly be seen in large schools near shallow rocky reefs, where they graze on the rock surfaces. Its range extends from the Gulf of California to the coast of El Salvador and the Revillagigedo Islands.

370. *Prionurus laticlavius* Valenciennes, the Galapagos surgeonfish, is a schooling fish, as can be seen by this photo. Note that the fish do not have the multitude of spots found in *P. punctatus*. This species may at times be referred to as *Xesurus laticlavius*. Photo taken in the Galapagos by Taylor Caffery.

371. *Prionurus punctatus* Gill, the spotted surgeonfish, is also a schooling species. It differs from *P. laticlavius* by having a completely spotted body and head. Photo by Alex Kerstitch of adults about 35 cm in length at a depth of 28 meters at Cabo San Lucas, Baja California, Mexico.

372. A very small juvenile (about 4 cm) spotted surgeonfish. The adult pattern is evident even at this size. Photo by Alex Kerstitch of a specimen from Baja California, Mexico.

373. Juveniles have two color patterns, the second a brilliant yellow. This juvenile apparently has been caught between the two phases. Photo by Dr. R. E. Thresher at Punta Pescadero, Gulf of California.

374. *Zanclus canescens* (Linnaeus), the Moorish idol, is said to often accompany black-nosed butterflyfish, as shown in this photo. The Moorish idol is basically an Indo-Pacific species. Photo by Alex Kerstitch at a depth of 18 meters at Cabo San Lucas, Baja California, Mexico.

Family SCORPAENIDAE
SCORPIONFISHES and ROCKFISHES

The Scorpaenidae is a fairly large family of some 400 species included in about 50 genera, over 100 of the species belonging to the single genus *Sebastes*. Most species inhabit temperate marine waters, with a few from tropical areas (including a few that are found in tropical rivers). Scorpionfishes and rockfishes remain at or near the bottom in rocky areas (hence the name rockfishes) at depths extending from a few centimeters to over 450 meters. In our area of coverage the genus *Sebastes* dominates with approximately 65 species, some 60 of which are found on the long, temperate coastline of the state of California.

Scorpionfishes and rockfishes are somewhat bass-like in form with a large (usually spiny) head, a large mouth, and large pectoral fins. Characteristic also is a bony suborbital stay (ridge) below the eye across the cheek. The size of adults ranges from about 15 cm to a few large species over 90 cm in length. Most species are cryptically colored with reds and browns predominating, although some species are brightly, even gaudily, colored.

Scorpionfishes are so-called because of their poisonous dorsal, anal, and pelvic spines, which can cause (depending upon which species is involved) very painful or even fatal stings. Although the worst offenders are found in tropical Indo-Pacific waters (especially species of the genus *Pterois*), at least one of the species in our area of coverage (*Scorpaena guttata*) is said to be almost as virulent.

Fertilization is internal in all species, but a few species lay eggs instead of giving live birth. *Scorpaena guttata*, for example, is one of the few species in the family that is not ovoviviparous. It lays eggs embedded in the thin walls of a paired gelatinous balloon-like

375. *Sebastes atrovirens* (Jordan & Gilbert), the kelp rockfish, has a range that extends from central California to central Baja California. It is usually seen at depths to 46 meters but is most common at a range of 9 to 12 meters. Photo by Ken Lucas at Steinhart Aquarium.

376. The kelp rockfish in its natural habitat, usually at or near the bottom around rocks or kelp. Photo by Daniel W. Gotshall at Santa Barbara, California.

377. *Sebastes auriculatus* Girard, the brown rockfish, also prefers rocky areas. It has a range from southeastern Alaska to central Baja California. Photo by Daniel W. Gotshall at Santo Tomas, Baja California.

378. One of the distinguishing marks of the brown rockfish is the dark brown blotch at the posterior portion of the gill cover. Photo by Ken Lucas at Steinhart Aquarium.

379. *Sebastes carnatus* (Jordan & Gilbert), the gopher rockfish, has a number of flesh-colored areas on the body giving the species a mottled appearance. Photo by Ken Lucas at Steinhart Aquarium.

380. The gopher rockfish prefers rocky areas in depths to over 50 meters. This territorial species is more common below 15 meters. Photo of a 40-cm individual by Dr. Gerald R. Allen at Steinhart Aquarium.

381. *Sebastes caurinus* Richardson, the copper rockfish, occurs in rocky areas to depths of about 180 meters. Photo by Daniel W. Gotshall at Point Lobos (Whaler's Cove), California.

382. An adult copper rockfish. The color is variable to some extent. The white area following the lateral line is said to be more noticeable when the fish is excited. Photo by Ken Lucas at Steinhart Aquarium.

383. A younger copper rockfish about 10 cm long. The species ranges from the Gulf of Alaska to central Baja California. Photo by Dr. Gerald R. Allen at Steinhart Aquarium.

384. *Sebastes chrysomelas* (Jordan & Gilbert), the black-and-yellow rockfish, in its natural habitat. It occurs in rocky areas down to 37 meters but is most common above 18 meters. Photo by Daniel W. Gotshall at Diablo Canyon, California.

385. *Sebastes chrysomelas* resembles the gopher rockfish, but the pale areas are distinctly yellow in the black-and-yellow rockfish. Photo by Ken Lucas at Steinhart Aquarium.

386. *Sebastes constellatus* (Jordan & Gilbert), the starry rockfish, derives its common name from the bright white spots on the body, both big and small. Photo by Al Engasser.

387. Starry rockfish inhabit deep reefs from about 25 to over 270 meters, where they are occasionally caught by fishermen. Photo by Ken Lucas at Steinhart Aquarium.

388. *Sebastes flavidus* (Ayres), the yellowtail rockfish, has a range from Kodiak Island, Alaska, to southern California. It is commonly found in pelagic schools feeding on fishes and crustaceans. Photo by Daniel W. Gotshall at Monterey, California.

389. *Sebastes entomelas* (Jordan & Gilbert), the widow rockfish, often occurs in schools at 25 to over 30 meters depth. The young are found in shallower water. Photo by Daniel W. Gotshall.

390. *Sebastes dalli* (Eigenmann & Beeson), the calico rockfish, is a rather small species usually less than 20 cm in length. This pleasingly patterned species extends from San Francisco to central Baja California. Photo by Daniel W. Gotshall at Quart Reef, California.

391. *Sebastes hopkinsi* (Cramer), the squarespot rockfish, is another smallish species usually less than 25 cm. It prefers shallow reefs between 18 and 180 meters. Photo by Daniel W. Gotshall.

392. *Sebastes maliger* (Jordan & Gilbert), the quillback rockfish, attains a length of about 60 cm. It occurs among rocks to over 270 meters depth. Photo by Daniel W. Gotshall at Vancouver Island, British Columbia, Canada.

393. *Sebastes maliger* has a range that extends from the Gulf of Alaska to central California. In the northern part of its range it is generally found in shallower waters. Photo by Al Engasser.

394. The quillback rockfish is aptly named, as can be seen in this photo showing the dorsal spines partially erect. The deeply notched membranes between the spines enhance the spiny nature of the fin. Photo by Ken Lucas at Steinhart Aquarium.

395. *Sebastes melanops* Girard, the black rockfish, occurs both in open water near the surface and near the bottom at depths to more than 360 meters. Photo of a 12-cm individual by Alex Kerstitch.

396. A black rockfish more than twice the size of the individual pictured above. The species attains a size of 60 cm. Photo of a 25-cm individual taken by Dr. Gerald R. Allen at Steinhart Aquarium.

397. *Sebastes miniatus* (Jordan & Gilbert), the vermilion rockfish, has a depth range to about 275 meters. The deeper-living individuals usually are redder in color. Photo by Daniel W. Gotshall.

398. *Sebastes mystinus* (Jordan & Gilbert), the blue rockfish, extends along the coast from British Columbia (possibly Alaska) to northern Baja California. It attains a length of about 50 cm. Photo by Dr. Gerald R. Allen at Steinhart Aquarium.

399. The blue rockfish is a schooling species that lives off the bottom and feeds mainly on krill. It may even school with other species of rockfishes. Photo by Dr. Gerald R. Allen at Steinhart Aquarium.

400. *Sebastes nebulosus* Ayres, the China rockfish, in its natural habitat among the inshore rocks and reefs. In contrast to the schooling species, this rockfish is territorial. Photo by Daniel W. Gotshall at a depth of 20 meters at Point Pinos.

401. The China rockfish is quite colorful, with yellowish white mottling against blue-black. The white of the dorsal spine(s) often connects with the pale stripe following the course of the lateral line. Photo by Ken Lucas at Steinhart Aquarium.

402. *Sebastes nigrocinctus* Ayres, the tiger rockfish, will vigorously defend its home, usually a cave or crevice among the rocks. This solitary species has a depth range between 50 and 275 meters. Photo by Daniel W. Gotshall at Vancouver Island, British Columbia.

403. The tiger rockfish is quite colorful, with five dark red bars on a pinkish to orange background. The species attains a length of about 60 cm. Photo by Dr. Gerald R. Allen of a 35-cm individual at Steinhart Aquarium.

404. *Sebastes paucispinis* Ayres, the bocaccio, inhabits rocky areas between 25 and 320 meters. Juveniles, such as the one seen here, are usually found in shallower water than are adults. Photo by Daniel W. Gotshall.

405. An adult bocaccio. This species attains a length of just over 90 cm and is said to live to 30 years of age. It is highly predatory. Photo by Ken Lucas at Steinhart Aquarium.

406. *Sebastes pinniger* (Gill), the canary rockfish, has a range of from southeastern Alaska to northern Baja California at depths of 90 to 274 meters. Photo by Alex Kerstitch of an individual about 18 cm in length.

407. The canary rockfish is well marked with orange on a gray-white background. The lateral line is usually in a pale area. This species feeds on small fishes and krill. Photo by Ken Lucas at Steinhart Aquarium.

408. *Sebastes rastrelliger* (Jordan & Gilbert), the grass rockfish, occurs in a variety of habitats, including rocky areas, kelp, and eelgrass beds. It is not colorful, being mostly greenish or olive in color. Photo by Daniel W. Gotshall.

409. *Sebastes rosaceus* Girard, the rosy rockfish, usually is found along the California coast to central Baja California and possibly north to the state of Washington. Photo of a pair of 23-cm individuals by Dr. Gerald R. Allen at Steinhart Aquarium.

410. The rosy rockfish is quite colorful and easily recognized by the pattern of white spots on a background of golden and pinkish violet. Photo by Ken Lucas at Steinhart Aquarium.

411. A younger rosy rockfish swimming among the invertebrates of a tank at Steinhart Aquarium. The fish seen behind the head of the rosy rockfish is *Chirolophis decoratus*. Photo by Ken Lucas.

412. *Sebastes ruberrimus* (Cramer), the yelloweye rockfish, undergoes color changes with growth. This juvenile has two pale stripes on the side of the body and head. Photo by Daniel W. Gotshall.

413. The yelloweye rockfish loses the lower stripe with age. It grows quite large, attaining a length of 90 cm, and the second stripe eventually also disappears. Photo by Daniel W. Gotshall.

414. A fully adult rosy rockfish. The natural habitat is rocky areas between 45 and 550 meters. Its range is from the Gulf of Alaska to northern Baja California. Photo by Ken Lucas at Steinhart Aquarium.

415. *Sebastes rubrivinctus* (Jordan & Gilbert), the flag rockfish, has a limited range extending from San Francisco to northern Baja. It prefers rocky areas. Photo by Dr. Gerald R. Allen at Steinhart Aquarium.

416. A young flag rockfish at a depth of 55 meters. The species occurs between 30 and 183 meters. Photo by Daniel W. Gotshall at Catalina Island, California.

417. The flag rockfish has the predorsal red band extending down to the gill cover. A related species, *S. babcocki* has it curving back to the pectoral fin base. Photo by Ken Lucas at Steinhart Aquarium.

418. *Sebastes serranoides* (Eigenmann & Eigenmann), the olive rockfish, occurs at various depths from the surface to over 140 meters, sometimes
away from the bottom as seen in this photo. Photo by Daniel W. Gotshall
at a depth of 30 meters at Point Lobos.

419. The olive rockfish ranges from northern California to central Baja California. It is an important sports fish,
as are many of the other rockfishes. Photo by Dr. Herbert R. Axelrod.

420. *Sebastes serriceps* (Jordan & Gilbert), the treefish, has juveniles with a great deal of yellow speckling almost obscuring the characteristic banding. The brittle stars help indicate the size of the fish. Photo of a 15-cm individual by Alex Kerstitch.

421. A slightly larger treefish showing some color changes. The treefish prefers rocky areas in depths to about 45 meters. Photo by Ken Lucas at Steinhart Aquarium.

422. An adult treefish. The species attains a size of about 40 cm and is said to be territorial. Note the "V"-shaped posterior marking and the bars extending onto the base of the dorsal fin. Photo by Daniel W. Gotshall.

423. In this juvenile treefish the bars are all but obliterated, making the fish look quite different from the adult shown above. Photo of a juvenile by Ken Lucas at Steinhart Aquarium.

424. *Sebastes umbrosus* (Jordan & Gilbert), the honeycomb rockfish, is a relatively small species (to 27 cm) occurring on or near the bottom as seen here. Photo of a juvenile by Daniel W. Gotshall at a depth of about 55 meters at Bird Rock, Catalina.

425. An adult honeycomb rockfish. The species occurs from central California to south-central Baja California but is more common in the central and southern parts of this range. Photo by Ken Lucas at Steinhart Aquarium.

426. *Scorpaena guttata* Girard, the California scorpionfish, in its natural habitat, which usually consists of rocks where it can blend in with the background. Photo by Daniel W. Gotshall.

427. The California scorpionfish lives up to its name with venomous fin spines that can inflict a painful wound. Photo by Ken Lucas at Steinhart Aquarium.

428. *Scorpaena plumieri mystes* Jordan & Starks, the stone scorpionfish, is seen here doing its best imitation of a rock in its natural habitat. Photo of an individual of about 38 cm by Alex Kerstitch at Guaymas, Sonora, Mexico.

429. *Scorpaena plumieri mystes* may eventually be called *S. mystes* if it is determined to be a full species. This is a deep-water color form. Photo by Alex Kerstitch of an adult (24 cm) from 30 meters at Morro Colorado, Mexico.

430. Another unusual color variation of the stone scorpionfish. This one, of about 15 cm length, was photographed by Alex Kerstitch at Guaymas, Sonora, Mexico.

431. A typical *Scorpaena plumieri mystes* pattern, although this is a small specimen (10 cm) and the species attains a maximum length of about 46 cm. Photo of a specimen from Panama by Dr. Gerald R. Allen.

432. *Scorpaenodes xyris* (Jordan & Gilbert), the rainbow scorpionfish, has a range that extends from southern California to Peru. It is a small species (to about 7.6 cm). Photo of a 7.5-cm individual by Alex Kerstitch at Guaymas, Sonora, Mexico.

433. The rainbow scorpionfish is readily identifiable by the prominent dark brown spot at the posterior lower edge of the gill cover. Photo by Dr. Gerald R. Allen of a specimen from Panama.

434. *Sebastolobus alascanus* Bean, the shortspine thornyhead, is common in deep water (26 to more than 1,500 meters) on a soft bottom. Photo by Daniel W. Gotshall of a specimen from Eureka, California.

435. *Scorpaena sonorae* Jenkins & Evermann, the Sonora scorpionfish, is a species associated with sandy bottoms. Note the large eye in comparison with the other species of *Scorpaena*. Photo by Alex Kerstitch of a 9.5-cm specimen from Morro Colorado, Sonora, Mexico.

structure (representing the paired ovaries?).

Some species of scorpaenids are fished commercially. In rocky areas the major method of capture is by hook-and-line, but trawls are used in deeper waters where the bottom is relatively free from rocks.

The kelp rockfish, *Sebastes atrovirens*, usually inhabits kelp beds and has been seen by divers resting on the kelp. The aurora rockfish, *S. aurora*, is a bright pinkish red or orange-red species usually trawled on soft bottoms to over 750 meters depth; specimens that lose scales in the trawl are more whitish because the empty scale pockets are white bordered by red. *Sebastes flavidus*, the yellowtail rockfish, is unusual in that it is mostly pelagic, commonly occurring in schools at depths of 25 to 50 meters (although it sometimes occurs from near the surface to over 250 meters in depth); it feeds on pelagic fishes and crustaceans. The black rockfish, *Sebastes melanops*, departs from the usual red or brown hues, being blackish or blue-black mottled with gray; it lives both on and off the bottom, often in schools, and makes up a good part of the party boat catches. One of the more colorful rockfishes is the tiger rockfish, *Sebastes nigrocinctus*, a species with five dark reddish black bars on a pinkish to red ground color; it is solitary and defends a territory, usually a rock crevice at depths of 50 to 270 meters.

The bocaccio, *S. paucispinis*, is a wide-ranging species that also has a wide depth range (found from 25 to over 300 meters). The adults are voracious predators (rockfishes in general are important reef predators) feeding mostly on fishes. Although adults are only rarely caught on hook-and-line, the young school and are hooked more commonly over rocky areas. This species is said to reach an age of 30 years. Large females may contain more than two million eggs.

436. An unidentified scorpionfish that was photographed by Ken Lucas at the Steinhart Aquarium.

Family TRIGLIDAE
SEAROBINS

The unusual and often highly colored searobins are bottom fishes found from fairly shallow waters to moderate depths in tropical and temperate areas. The head is quite bony and casque-like and is usually also provided with several spines and ridges. There are two dorsal fins (an anterior spiny fin and a posterior soft-rayed one) and a split pectoral fin. The upper portion of the pectoral fin is large and fan-like and is used for swimming; the lower portion is composed of several separate rays (usually three) that are used as feelers for probing for food as well as for turning over small stones or other debris in their search for food. These lower rays may also be brought into play as the searobin "walks" along the bottom.

Searobins are considered good food fishes in certain areas, and fishermen have noted that these fishes produce sounds when captured. They apparently also produce sounds when mating, for the sounds made by the males are more intense at the time of the breeding season. A second, different sound generated (a "vibrant grunt" as opposed to the "staccato call" of the breeding males) is theorized to be a warning or alarm call. In species where life history information is available the eggs are pelagic, varying from 1.0 to 1.7 mm in diameter (depending upon species).

437. *Bellator gymnostethus* (Gilbert) is a small species (to about 9 cm) that has been taken in the Gulf of California in shallow water over sandy bottoms. Photo by Alex Kerstitch of a 7.5-cm individual from Guaymas, Sonora, Mexico.

Family ANOPLOPOMATIDAE
SABLEFISH and SKILFISH

The Anoplopomatidae is a small family containing only two genera, each with a single species. Both the sablefish, *Anoplopoma fimbria*, and the skilfish, *Erilepis zonifer*, are from the North Pacific and both are from relatively deep water as adults—the sablefish to 1500 meters, the skilfish to 450 meters—although the juveniles may be found near the surface. The skilfish attains a length of about two meters while the sablefish attains only half that size. Both are streamlined fishes with two dorsal fins, the first dorsal being composed entirely of spines and the second with one or two spines followed by 15 to 20 soft rays. The flesh of the sablefish is reported to be very good eating (excellent when smoked), and it is fished for commercially.

Spawning in the sablefish apparently occurs during the winter when pelagic, smooth, 2 mm diameter eggs are released. By May juveniles about 2.5 cm long are found at the surface. Large schools of juveniles are also reported to appear in inshore harbors and inlets. As a result of tagging programs, it is known that this species makes extensive migrations of up to 2700 miles.

The natural food of the sablefish includes crustaceans, worms, and small fishes. In captivity it is not particular about its diet and will accept a reasonable variety of available foods.

The skilfish apparently has similar habits. It is said to thrive in captivity, and the Vancouver Aquarium reports one grew from 25 cm to just over 100 cm in a period of ten years.

438. *Anoplopoma fimbria* (Pallas), the sablefish, is a widely distributed migratory species with a range from Japan to central Baja California. Adults occur at depths of from 300 to over 1,800 meters on mud bottoms; juveniles are found in shallower water. Photo by Daniel W. Gotshall of an individual from Eureka, California.

Family HEXAGRAMMIDAE
GREENLINGS

A small family of moderate to large fishes from the North Pacific, the hexagrammids are common bottom fishes that are mostly encountered in shallow water, but at least one species extends to more than 400 meters in depth. The dorsal fin is moderately to deeply notched (the division is between the spinous and soft portions of the dorsal) and in species of *Zaniolepis* several anterior spines are moderately to greatly elongate. In at least one species of this last genus the anal fin is notched along with the dorsal. *Zaniolepis* has, in fact, additional differences from the other Hexagrammidae such as the presence of comb-like scales, unperforated scales in the lateral line, and a number of internal characters. These differences have led certain workers to regard *Zaniolepis* as belonging to its own family, the Zaniolepidae. The longspine combfish (*Zaniolepis latipinnis*) and the shortspine combfish (*Z. frenata*) are said to exhibit peculiar behavior

immediately after being dumped on deck from a trawl: they will take their tails into their mouths, forming an "O". As yet there has been no explanation for this possibly defensive maneuver.

Oxylebius pictus, the painted greenling, is quite distinctive with its pattern of dark red bars on a tan to gray ground color and has often been referred to by the common name convict fish because of this pattern. Males are said to have some black showing through the pattern, including the red bars. It is most often encountered in rocky habitats, where it can be seen hanging vertically on the steep rocky faces, a habit that is also exhibited in captivity. This species also seems to be immune to the stinging cells of the anemone *Tealia*, which is quite common in the same habitat, and individuals can sometimes be seen resting among the tentacles of this anemone. The diet consists of a variety of invertebrates, including crustaceans, polychaetes, small molluscs, and bryozoans, with the crustaceans and worms generally preferred. Spawning is said to occur at least from

439. *Hexagrammos* sp. Greenlings are coldwater fishes with a distribution restricted to the North Pacific. Most species have more than one lateral line, and some species are sexually dichromatic. Photo of a 35-cm individual by Dr. Gerald R. Allen at Steinhart Aquarium.

440. *Hexagrammos decagrammus* (Pallas), the kelp greenling, is one of the sexually dimorphic species. Shown here is the freckled female. This species occurs from Alaska to southern California. Photo by Ken Lucas at Steinhart Aquarium.

441. The kelp greenling inhabits rocky shores, kelp beds, and even sandy bottoms to a depth of about 50 meters. Photo of a female by Daniel W. Gotshall.

February through November and may occur year 'round. Clusters of orange-colored eggs are deposited among low-growing algae on the rocky substrate, to which they adhere. The male at this time is very aggressive toward all other animals (including skin divers), attacking them if they come too near; he is apparently guarding the eggs, but his duties end as soon as the eggs hatch. No information is available regarding the number of eggs and the time it takes for them to hatch. Painted greenlings are said to make very good aquarium inhabitants.

The kelp greenling, *Hexagrammos decagrammus*, attains a length of over 50 cm and is distributed from Alaska to the southern part of California. There is considerable sexual dimorphism, with the male sporting a number of blue spots each surrounded by a ring of reddish brown spots. Spawning apparently occurs in the fall, when large masses of pale blue eggs are laid. Blue eggs are also characteristic of some other species of this genus.

442. The male kelp greenling is not freckled but is brownish (as seen here) to greenish gray (see photo below) with a number of blue spots, especially anteriorly. Photo by Daniel W. Gotshall.

443. The blue spots of the male, as shown here, are surrounded by a number of darker spots. The kelp greenling is prized as a sports fish. Photo by Ken Lucas at Steinhart Aquarium.

444. *Ophiodon elongatus,* the lingcod, is a highly rated food fish and is sought after by sports fishermen and commercial fishermen alike. Adults prefer rocky areas, whereas the young are more likely to be found on mud bottoms of inshore areas. Photo by Daniel W. Gotshall at Point Lobos, California.

445. The lingcod ranges from Kodiak Island, Alaska, to northern Baja California and from inshore waters to depths of 427 meters. The fish above the lingcod is a kelp rockfish. Photo by Daniel W. Gotshall at Monterey, California.

446. A closeup of the head of *Ophiodon elongatus*. This species is a voracious predator, feeding mainly on fishes. Photo by Ken Lucas at Steinhart Aquarium.

The lingcod, *Ophiodon elongatus*, grows quite large (up to 152 cm and 32 kg) and is commercially important. Because of its commercial value this species is better known than many of the other species of the family. Spawning takes place in the winter months (December to March), when the female will start to deposit a layer of eggs in a crevice or under a rock along with a yellowish viscous secretion that when in contact with water forms a binding agent, attaching the eggs to the rock surface. The male then swims over the eggs, fertilizing them. This procedure continues for about half an hour, during which time the surrounding water becomes quite cloudy. Up to 500,000 fairly large (2.8-3.5 mm) pinkish eggs are deposited and are guarded by the male as the female departs. The smaller, darker male continuously fans the egg mass by movements of his pectoral fins, both aerating them and keeping them free from any debris. Intruders are viciously attacked, being bitten or bumped until they move away and are no longer considered a threat to the eggs (usually a distance of several feet). A wooden speargun handle poked too near a guarding male was bitten, and the tooth marks were plainly visible afterward. The egg masses are large, to 76 cm across and weighing up to 14 kg, with the eggs on the outer surface hatching first (some fall prey to the "guarding" parent). The young are a little less than 1 cm in length and possess a bright yellow oil droplet and blue eyes. The yolk sac is absorbed in a week and a half, and the young may reach a length of almost 5 cm by April; yearlings are about 27 cm in length. Lingcod juveniles feed on copepods and other crustaceans, whereas the adults feed voraciously on fishes (herring, sand lance, cod, pollock, flounder, etc.), crustaceans, and octopuses and are even cannibalistic.

447. *Oxylebias pictus* Gill, the painted greenling, inhabits rocky areas down to a depth of about 50 meters from Kodiak Island, Alaska, to central Baja California. Photo by Ken Lucas at Steinhart Aquarium.

448. A painted greenling sitting seemingly unconcerned in an anemone, *Tealia* sp. This species attains a length of 25 cm but is not usually seen much over 15 cm. It is also known as the convict fish. Photo by Ken Lucas at Steinhart Aquarium.

449. *Zaniolepis latipinnis* Girard, the longspine combfish. *Zaniolepis* is sometimes included in the family Hexagrammidae and is sometimes set apart in its own family. Photo by Ken Lucas at Steinhart Aquarium.

450. A female painted greenling. The color pattern can change somewhat. Here it has become quite dark (although the banding is still evident) and numerous white spots are visible. Photo by Ken Lucas of a 20-cm individual at Steinhart Aquarium.

451. *Zaniolepis frenata* Eigenmann & Eigenmann, the shortspine combfish, does not actually have short anterior dorsal spines, but they are much shorter than those of the longspine combfish. Both species occur on soft bottoms. Photo by Ken Lucas at Steinhart Aquarium.

452. The shortspine combfish ranges from southern Oregon to central Baja California at depths between 55 and 244 meters. The skin is sandpaper-like. Photo by Ken Lucas at Steinhart Aquarium.

Family COTTIDAE
SCULPINS

The Cottidae is a fairly large (approximately 300 species) family of mostly bottom-dwelling fishes generally referred to as sculpins. They are mostly circumboreal in distribution, inhabiting marine, brackish, and even fresh waters. The dorsal fin is usually either deeply notched or divided into two separate fins, but there are several exceptions. The pectoral fins are generally quite large, with the lowermost rays sometimes partially to fully separated. The head may be quite smooth to extremely rugose, spiny, notched, or otherwise modified and is often provided with cirri or other appendages. The eyes are large and usually placed high on the head. The body shape is quite variable, from somewhat elongate and slender to very chunky, and the size range in the area covered is approximately 5 cm to over 75 cm.

One of the largest East Pacific sculpins is the cabezon, *Scorpaenichthys marmoratus*, which attains a length of about 75 cm and a weight of over 11 kg. Spawning occurs during the winter months (January through March), and the greenish eggs are attached to the rocks. The flesh is often greenish, too, but although the green flesh is good to eat the greenish eggs are definitely poisonous, possibly a defensive mechanism to protect them from animals and birds that can reach them at low tide. Food of the 1 cm young consists of copepods and other crustaceans and their larvae; food of older individuals consists mainly of crustaceans, with fishes and molluscs of lesser desirability.

In the longfin sculpin, *Jordania zonope*, breeding was observed in October. Both sexes, but especially the male, become darker in color, and a number of egg masses each containing 20-30 eggs are laid. This species is reported to be territorial in nature, and SCUBA divers have seen it hanging on vertical rock faces.

The wooly sculpin, *Clinocottus analis*, has a range that extends from Cape Mendocino in California to Asuncion Point in Baja California. It inhabits mostly the intertidal and shallow subtidal areas but is known to extend to depths of at least 18 meters. Little is known about the life history of the species, but a cluster of eggs numbering several hundred was found under rocks. They took over three weeks to hatch. Another species, *C. acuticeps*, is said to lay brown eggs about 1 mm in diameter and probably spawns in late spring or summer.

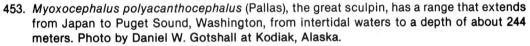

453. *Myoxocephalus polyacanthocephalus* (Pallas), the great sculpin, has a range that extends from Japan to Puget Sound, Washington, from intertidal waters to a depth of about 244 meters. Photo by Daniel W. Gotshall at Kodiak, Alaska.

454. *Jordania zonope* Starks, the longfin sculpin, inhabits rocky areas and kelp beds from southeastern Alaska to central California. Photo by Daniel W. Gotshall.

Artedius harringtoni, the scalyhead sculpin, is reported to exhibit sexual dimorphism, with the male possessing well developed plumose cirri that are not present in the female. There is also some sexual dichromatism, with the female having some white to pink or red on the anal and pelvic fins. Spawning by some members of the genus occurs in the summer while in others it occurs in the winter months. Eggs are generally deposited in protected areas and may be salmon-colored (*A. fenestralis*) to cherry-red (*A. lateralis*). In *A. fenestralis* the eggs are said to form low mounds in protected areas such as corners or rocky caves in aquaria. The males guard them, keeping them clean and well aerated with their pectoral fins. In *A. lateralis* they are similarly placed and hatch in about 16 days.

455. *Clinocottus analis* (Girard), the woolly sculpin, is a shallow-water species frequenting tidepools and intertidal areas to a depth of about 18 meters. Photo by Daniel W. Gotshall at San Nicolas, California.

The red Irish lord, *Hemilepidotus hemilepidotus*, is said to deposit masses of pink eggs in shallow or intertidal waters where they are easily seen. The buffalo sculpin, *Enophrys bison*, spawns in winter (February and March), depositing small clusters of brownish orange eggs. It has a threatening behavior involving the expansion of the gill covers to display the large spines of the preopercle and opercle. The diet of the buffalo sculpin includes such things as shrimp, crabs, and other crustaceans, fishes (herring, salmon, sand lance), mussels, and even sea lettuce (*Ulva*).

Perhaps the most unusual species of the family, at least from the aquarist's point of view, is the grunt sculpin, *Rhamphocottus richardsoni*. The common name arises from its ability to make grunting noises that are clearly audible when it is removed from the water. These small (7.6 cm) fish are awkward swimmers (usually in a head-high position) and are more usually seen moving across the bottom in a series of short jumps, aided by the separated finger-like lower rays of the pectoral fins. To further enhance its comical appearance, the eyes move independently. Spawning occurs in late summer to winter depending upon locality. Observations in aquaria indicate the female aggressively pursues the male until she corners him in a cave, corner, or other limited exit area. He is kept there until she deposits about 150 yellow to orange eggs and he fertilizes them. The eggs are slow to hatch, taking up to 20 weeks. Very small grunt sculpins (1.4-1.8 cm) have been captured in low salinity water. They were feeding on copepods and other crustaceans and their larvae as well as fish larvae. Grunt sculpins are common in tidal pools and on rocky coasts, where they are relatively easy to capture, but may also be found on sandy beaches and to depths of at least 165 meters. They do quite well in aquaria if the water temperature is kept below 13 °C and sufficient food (usually crustaceans) is available. They are said to survive in captivity for several years.

456. *Leiocottus hirundo* Girard, the lavender sculpin, is a colorful species with a limited range (southern California to northern Baja California). Photo by Daniel W. Gotshall.

457. *Artedius harringtoni* Starks, the scalyhead sculpin, is found in rocky areas and around pilings in intertidal and subtidal waters. Photo by Daniel W. Gotshall.

458. *Artedius corallinus* (Hubbs), the coralline sculpin, is fairly common in rocky areas in California, but its range extends to the state of Washington and to northern Baja California. Photo by Daniel W. Gotshall at Monterey, California.

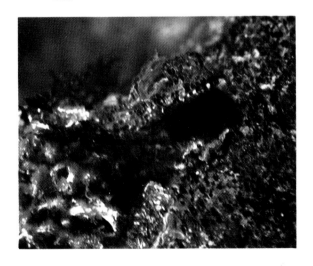

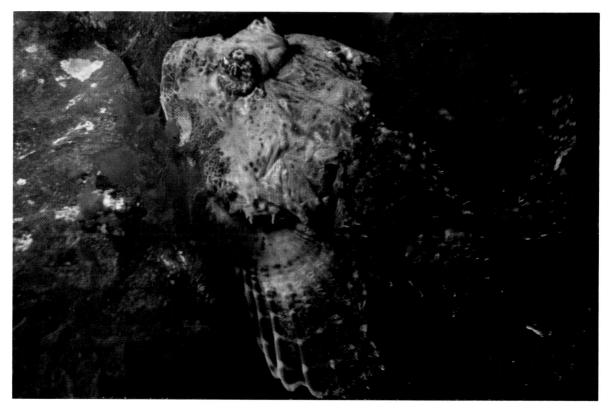

459. *Enophrys bison* (Girard), the buffalo sculpin, has large, plate-like lateral line scales and a long upper preopercular spine. Algae form a major part of the diet. Photo by Daniel W. Gotshall.

460. *Psychrolutes paradoxus* Guenther, the tadpole sculpin, is a small (to 6.4 cm), tadpole-like fish with a smooth head. It extends from the northern Sea of Japan to Puget Sound. Photo by Dr. Gerald R. Allen at Steinhart Aquarium.

461. *Hemilepidotus hemilepidotus* (Tilesius), the red Irish lord, in its natural habitat. Although it is usually found close to shore, it does have a depth range to 48 meters. Photo by Daniel W. Gotshall at Vancouver Island, British Columbia.

462. A close-up of the head of the red Irish lord. The notch between the third and fourth spines is evident. Photo by Dr. Gerald R. Allen of a 35-cm individual at Steinhart Aquarium.

463. *Scorpaenichthys marmoratus* (Ayres), the cabezon, is one of the most common sculpins on the California coast. It feeds on invertebrates, including crustaceans and molluscs, and is itself good eating (although its eggs are poisonous). Photo by Daniel W. Gotshall at Monterey, California.

464. The male cabezon guards the eggs as seen here. The large male (the species attains a length almost a meter) makes a rather substantial barrier to any fish intent on a caviar dinner. Photo by Daniel W. Gotshall at Monterey.

465. *Orthonopias triacis* Starks & Mann, the snubnose sculpin, is found in rocky areas from intertidal regions to depths of about 30 meters. Photo by Daniel W. Gotshall between 9 and 15 meters at the Monterey Breakwater, California.

466. *Scorpaenichthys marmoratus.* This close-up of the head shows the supraorbital cirri and the skin flaps on the snout. Photo by Dr. Gerald R. Allen of a 25-cm individual at Steinhart Aquarium.

467. *Rhamphocottus richardsoni* Guenther, the grunt sculpin, is one of the most
sought after of aquarium fishes from the East Pacific. It is a coldwater species
with a range from Japan to Alaska and down the coast to southern California.
Photo by Daniel W. Gotshall.

468. The grunt sculpin is so-called because of the peculiar grunting sounds it makes. It is reported that a ripe
female will chase the male around an aquarium until she has him trapped (in a rock cave for example), keeping him there until she lays her eggs. Photo by Ken Lucas at Steinhart Aquarium.

Family AGONIDAE
POACHERS and ALLIGATORFISHES

The agonids or poachers are small fishes from the cold waters of the North Pacific, some species extending as far south as the California coast. They are normally elongate and covered with rows of non-overlapping bony plates that are often provided with saw-toothed edges. Agonids are bottom fishes that may be found from tidal pools to considerable depths (about 1200 meters) but are more commonly encountered at moderate depths. There are usually two dorsal fins, a spinous dorsal and a soft dorsal, although the former may be absent in some species. The pectoral fins are large and fan-like, like those of scorpaenids, and at least the sturgeon poacher, *Agonus acipenserinus,* has been observed to swim mainly by undulating movements of these fins. In males the pelvic fins (which are reduced to a spine and only two rays) along with the second dorsal and anal fins are sometimes longer than those of the females. In the warty poacher, *Occella verrucosa,* the male is reported to have orange and yellow in the pelvic fins. Most species are less than 30 cm in length, the smallest being the pixie poacher, *Occella impi,* at about 2 cm. Among the food items in the diet of some poachers are crustaceans and marine worms.

Family CYCLOPTERIDAE
LUMPSUCKERS and SNAILFISHES

Lumpsuckers and snailfishes are small to medium sized fishes, about 50 of the 175 or so species inhabiting the North Pacific. Most species have pelvic fins modified into a sucking disc with which they cling to rocks on the bottom; a few lack the sucking disc and pelvic fins and may be pelagic. The pectoral fins are usually large, often with the ventralmost rays modified (separated or elongated into a lobe). The dorsal fin is also variable, from a single many-rayed fin to a deeply notched fin to one or two separate short fins. The body of lumpsuckers is usually globular, with or without large tubercles, while that of snailfishes is generally elongate with the dorsal fin long.

In the smooth lumpsucker, *Aptocyclus ventricosus,* the males are reported to guard their eggs, whereas in the abyssal snailfish (the only known specimen was collected at a depth of almost 3000 meters off Canada), *Careproctus ovigerum,* the male was found to be carrying in his mouth a large mass of developing eggs. Lumpsuckers and snailfishes are carnivorous, with the young of the showy snailfish, *Liparis pulchellus,* as well as a number of other species, feeding on small crustaceans such as cumaceans and amphipods, while the adults are more prone to feed on decapod crustaceans and various marine worms.

469. *Odontopyxis trispinosa* Lockington, the pygmy poacher, attains a length of only about 9.5 cm. It inhabits soft bottoms from southeastern Alaska to central Baja California at depths of 9 to 373 meters. Photo by Daniel W. Gotshall at Tanker Buoy Reef, Monterey, California.

470. In *Occella verrucosa* (Lockington), the warty poacher, males have bright orange and black pelvic fins as seen here. The breast area Is covered with knobby plates, hence the common name warty poacher. Photo by Daniel W. Gotshall at Eureka, California.

471. The warty poacher occurs on soft substrates in a depth range of 18 to 274 meters from Alaska to central California. Photo by Daniel W. Gotshall at Eureka, California.

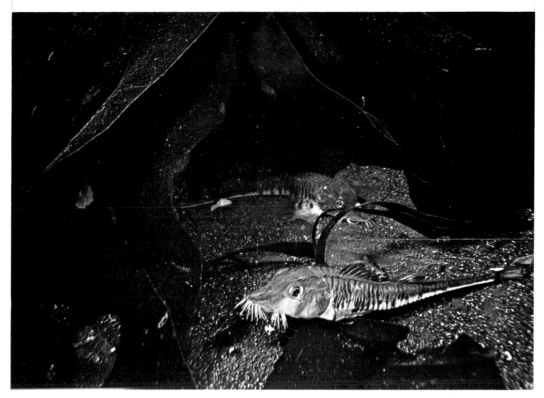

472. *Agonus acipenserinus* Tilesius, the sturgeon poacher, is easily recognized by the cluster of "whiskers" under the snout and at the corners of the mouth. It ranges from the Bering Sea to Eureka, California. Photo by Daniel W. Gotshall at Mill Bay, Kodiak, Alaska.

473. *Liparis pulchellus* Ayres, the showy snailfish, usually has a color pattern of wavy lines as seen here but may sometimes be plainly colored or even spotted. It ranges from the U.S.S.R. to Monterey Bay, California, and is usually found on soft bottoms. Photo by Daniel W. Gotshall.

Order PLEURONECTIFORMES
FLATFISHES

Flatfishes are quite unusual in that they spend their time lying on the bottom, one side always down, and have both eyes on the opposite (upper) side of the body. This is not always the case, for when they first hatch out from the egg they are fairly normal larvae. However, during their development one of the eyes migrates to the other side of the head of the fish so that both eyes are on the same side. In addition, the "blind" (bottom) side is usually pale or unpigmented (in contrast to the patterned upper side), the pectoral fins may become asymmetrical, the dorsal fin may extend forward onto the head, and even the mouth may become somewhat distorted. Whether the migrating eye moves to the right side of the fish (right-eyed) or to the left side (left-eyed) usually is of taxonomic importance, although there are exceptions. Included among the flatfishes in our area are the lefteye flounders (Bothidae), righteye flounders (Pleuronectidae), true soles (Soleidae), and tonguefishes (Cynoglossidae).

As the name suggests, the lefteye flounders (Bothidae) have the eyes and color on the left side. They are generally small to moderate sized fishes (most 30 cm or less) of some importance commercially. They often partially or almost completely bury themselves in the bottom sand, where they are virtually undetectable, for not only do their color and pattern resemble the substrate, but they can change color to a certain extent to enhance this resemblance. Natural food items are various crustaceans and fishes.

Included among the many species of the family are the sanddabs of the genus *Citharichthys*, some brightly patterned species of the genus *Bothus*, the fantail sole *Xystreurys liolepis* (not to be confused with the true soles), and other interesting species. Sex differences in some species include size of

474. *Citharichthys gilberti* Jenkins & Evermann, the Panamic sanddab, occurs from Guaymas to Panama and is said to ascend freshwater streams. Its Atlantic twin is *C. spilopterus.* Photo by Alex Kerstitch at a depth of 4.5 meters from Guaymas, Mexico.

475. *Citharichthys sordidus* Girard, the Pacific sanddab, has the eyes and color on the left side. This species occurs on sand bottoms from the Bering Sea to southern Baja California. Photo by Daniel W. Gotshall.

476. *Citharichthys stigmaeus* Jordan & Gilbert, the speckled sanddab, occurs on sand bottoms usually shallower than 90 meters (although it has been collected to over 300 meters). Photo by Ken Lucas at Steinhart Aquarium.

477. *Bothus leopardus* (Guenther), the leopard flounder, has its eyes and color on the left side. The color pattern is very distinctive and has earned it the common name of leopard flounder. Photo by Alex Kerstitch of a 20-cm individual off Punta Chivato, Baja California, Mexico.

478. *Paralichthys woolmani* Jordan & Williams, the Panamic peacock flounder, was originally discovered in the Galapagos Islands by the *Albatross* expedition, but it ranges up to the Gulf of California. Photo by Alex Kerstitch of an 80-cm specimen from Guaymas, Sonora, Mexico.

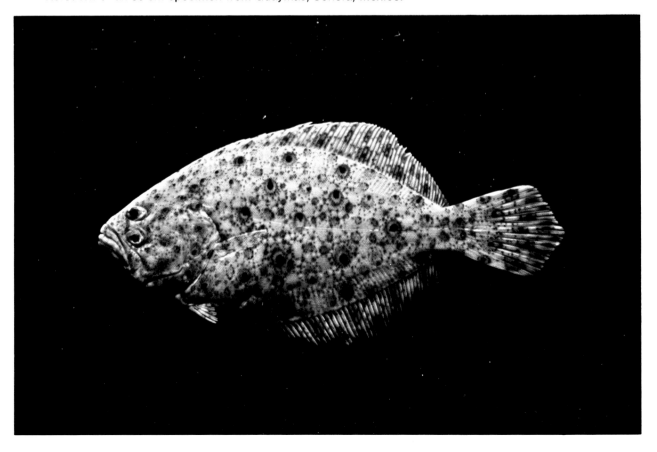

479. *Xystreurys liolepis* Jordan & Gilbert, the fantail sole, usually has eyes and pattern on the left side, but it is frequently right-eyed as seen here. Photo by Alex Kerstitch of a 7.3-cm specimen from Guaymas, Sonora, Mexico.

480. *Platichthys stellatus* (Pallas), the starry flounder, is a common flounder that occurs mostly near shore. It will enter brackish estuaries and perhaps even fresh water. Photo by Ken Lucas at Steinhart Aquarium.

481. *Lepidopsetta bilineata* (Ayres), the rock sole, is right-eyed and ranges from the Sea of Japan to southern California. It occurs on more of a pebbly substrate than do most flatfishes. Photo by Daniel W. Gotshall at Kodiak, Alaska.

482. *Psettichthys melanostictus* Girard, the sand sole, has some almost free rays at the beginning of the dorsal fin that help distinguish the species. It occurs from the Bering Sea to southern California. Photo by Ken Lucas at Steinhart Aquarium.

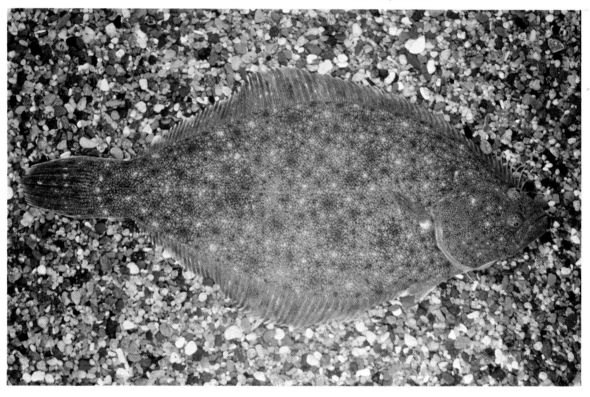

483. *Pleuronichthys verticalis* Jordan & Gilbert, the hornyhead turbot, is a right-eyed species, but the first few rays of the dorsal fin are on the blind (left) side. It occurs on soft substrates from central California to the Gulf of California. Photo by Alex Kerstitch of a 12-cm specimen trawled in 60 meters at Morro Colorado, Sonora, Mexico.

484. *Pleuronichthys ocellatus* Starks & Thompson, the ocellated turbot, was described from specimens collected in the Gulf of California. Photo by Alex Kerstitch of a 6.7-cm specimen from Guaymas, Sonora, Mexico.

485. *Pleuronichthys decurrens* Jordan & Gilbert, the curlfin turbot, is a common species occurring on soft substrates from Alaska to central Baja California. In California it is a commercial species used mostly for mink food. Photo by Daniel W. Gotshall at Locens Point at a depth of about 18 meters.

486. *Pleuronichthys coenosus* Girard, the C-O sole, is so-called because of the pattern on the caudal fin (an arc and circle combination). It occurs from southeastern Alaska to northern Baja California. Photo by Dr. Gerald R. Allen at Steinhart Aquarium.

the pectoral fins (longer in males than in females) and distance between the eyes (female closer). The eggs are pelagic and usually about a millimeter in diameter.

The righteye flounders (Pleuronectidae) include small to quite large fishes, some of the latter of great commercial importance. Most are marine fishes, although there are exceptions. The Pacific starry flounder (*Platichthys stellatus*), for example, is commonly found in brackish water and even enters areas of purely fresh water. It spawns in shallow water, releasing pale orange eggs about 1 mm in diameter. The larvae feed on copepods, barnacle larvae, and cladocerans, whereas adults tend toward crabs, shrimp, worms, clams, other small molluscs, brittle-stars, and small fishes. Also unusual for a flatfish species is the fact that the eyes and color may be on either side.

The Pacific halibut, *Hippoglossus stenolepis*, grows quite large, with females recorded to 267 cm and over 200 kg and males to 140 cm. It spawns in winter at depths of 275 to over 400 m, releasing 2-3 million 3.0-3.5 mm diameter eggs. Eggs and larvae remain in the open waters up to five months. Newly hatched larvae are about 1.1 cm long. The left eye starts migrating at a size of 1.8 cm. At about 3 cm this migration is completed and the larvae resemble the adults, although they are still pelagic. By six to seven months they are carried inshore. Food consists of crabs and other crustaceans, clams, squids, and fishes.

The true soles have the eyes on the right side of the head and usually quite close together. The preopercular margin is not free but is hidden under the skin. (Many species of Pleuronectidae are commonly called "soles," especially commercial species.) Most are marine species, although several species migrate into pure fresh water. In the East Pacific the soles are represented by a few species of lined soles (*Achirus*) and hogchokers (*Trinectes*) very similar to those occasionally found in petshops. Seldom more than a few centimeters long, these little soles are found in coastal, brackish, and even fresh waters from Sonora south.

The tonguefishes (Cynoglossidae) have the eyes and pattern on the left side, and the dorsal, anal, and caudal fins are united around the posterior end of the body. Pectoral fins are absent. The tonguefishes are small (usually less than 30 cm) and teardrop-shaped. The eyes are tiny and close-set.

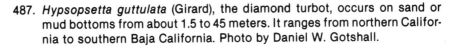
487. *Hypsopsetta guttulata* (Girard), the diamond turbot, occurs on sand or mud bottoms from about 1.5 to 45 meters. It ranges from northern California to southern Baja California. Photo by Daniel W. Gotshall.

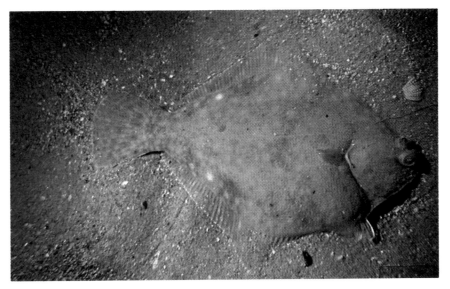

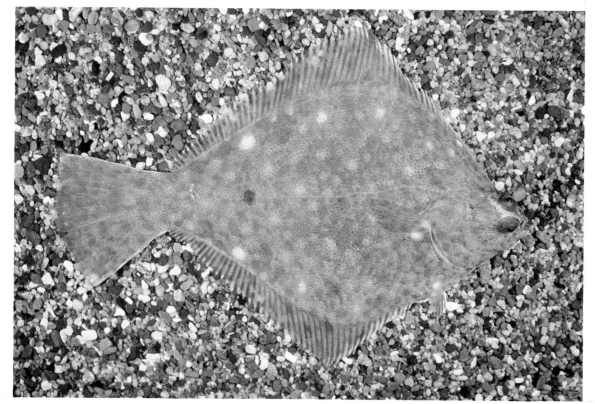

488. The diamond turbot receives its common name from the characteristic shape caused by the elongate middle rays of the dorsal and anal fins. Photo by Ken Lucas at Steinhart Aquarium.

489. *Microstomus pacificus* (Lockington), the Dover sole, occurs on mud bottoms between 18 and 914 meters. It is said to be slimy and very slippery to handle. Photo by Daniel W. Gotshall at 37 meters at Palos Verdes, California.

490. *Symphurus elongatus* (Guenther), the Panamic tonguefish, has a distribution from the Gulf of California along the Pacific coast to Central America. Photo by Alex Kerstitch of a specimen from Sonora, Mexico.

Order TETRAODONTIFORMES
PLECTOGNATHS

The Tetraodontiformes is an odd assemblage of related families (about ten in number), among which are included the triggerfishes and filefishes (Balistidae), puffers (Tetraodontidae), trunkfishes and boxfishes (Ostraciidae), porcupinefishes (Diodontidae), and ocean sunfishes (Molidae). They may be naked (but with a leathery skin), although most are provided with some kind of armor that may be in the form of bony shields or plates, prickles, or spines. Most species have a small mouth (which may be provided with strong teeth or beak-like jaws) and small gill openings without free opercles. They are normally encountered near shore (although some species are pelagic) in tropical or subtropical waters (a few species reach temperate areas). Some species pro-

duce a toxin in the body that can be fatal to humans if the fish is eaten; others release a substance when they are stressed that can be fatal to fishes trapped in the same aquarium.

The family Balistidae is now considered to include not only the triggerfishes but also the filefishes (formerly Monacanthidae) as well, the family total of species now about 120. The first dorsal fin is composed of two to three spines, the first spine with a locking mechanism that can be released by a trigger involving the second spine. The skin is thick and covered with large plate-like or rough scales, and some species have been given the common name "leatherjackets." Less than a dozen species are commonly seen in our area.

The species of the family Ostraciidae are called boxfishes because the body is enclosed in a rigid trunk-like dermal carapace or "box" with openings for the fins, eyes,

491. *Aluterus scriptus* (Osbeck), the scrawled filefish, occurs around the world in tropical waters. It is a fairly common fish in many parts of its range but is only occasionally seen in the Gulf of California. Photo by Alex Kerstitch of an individual of about 35 cm at a depth of 26 meters at Cabo San Lucas, Baja California, Mexico.

492. *Balistes polylepis* Steindachner, the finescale triggerfish, has a wide range (northern California to Chile) and occurs over rocky and sandy bottoms. Aggregations like this may be seen during the day around rocky or reefy areas. Photo by Alex Kerstitch at a depth of 20 meters at Window Rocks, Sonora, Mexico.

493. *Pseudobalistes naufragium* (Jordan & Starks), the blunthead triggerfish, is a more tropical species. Although it ranges from the Gulf of California to Ecuador, it is less common in the cooler areas. Photo by Alex Kerstitch at a depth of 12 meters at Isla Fralloa, Sinaloa, Mexico.

494. *Arothron meleagris* (Bloch & Schneider), the guineafowl or golden puffer, is an Indo-Pacific species whose range extends to the eastern Pacific from Guaymas to Ecuador. This is the normal spotted pattern. Photo by Dr. Gerald R. Allen of a 15-cm individual at Steinhart Aquarium.

495. A guineafowl puffer about to become a golden puffer. This individual has been caught in its transitional color phase between the spotted form and the golden form. Photo by Alex Kerstitch at a depth of about 4.5 meters at Cabo Pulmo, Baja California.

496. The rare golden form of *Arothron meleagris.* The species is said to feed on live corals and coral-associated animals in the Indo-Pacific. Photo by Alex Kerstitch at a depth of 4.5 meters at Pulmo Reef, Baja California, Mexico.

497. *Canthigaster punctatissima* (Guenther), the spotted sharpnose puffer, ranges from Guaymas to Panama and the Galapagos Islands. Photo by Dr. Gerald R. Allen of a 5-cm individual at a depth of 5 meters in Panama.

498. An adult spotted sharpnose puffer of about 7.5 cm. Note the difference in the spotting patterns between this specimen and the individual on the opposite page. Photo by Alex Kerstitch at a depth of 4.5 meters at San Carlos, Sonora, Mexico.

499. *Sphoeroides annulatus* (Jenyns), the bullseye puffer, occurs from southern California to Peru. It is found mostly over sandy bottoms, although it is not restricted to that substrate. Photo by Alex Kerstitch of a 9.6-cm specimen from Guaymas, Sonora, Mexico.

500. *Sphoeroides* sp., possibly *S. lobatus* (Steindachner). *S. lobatus* has skin flaps along its sides like the individual shown. Photo by Alex Kerstitch of a 20-cm individual at a depth of about 33 meters at Isla San Pedro Nolasco, Sonora, Mexico.

501. This *Mola mola* (Linnaeus), the ocean sunfish, looks like it is attempting to have itself cleaned by a pair of sharpnose surfperches *(Phanerodon atripes)*. Photo by Daniel Gotshall at Monterey, California.

502. The ocean sunfish is one of the most unusual of fishes, with a very truncated posterior end. It includes in its diet mostly jellyfishes, along with occasional fishes and algae. Photo by Daniel W. Gotshall at Monterey, California.

mouth, gill openings, nostrils, and anus. They are poor swimmers, propelling themselves by means of their tail and pectoral fins. They rely on the armor for protection, some species enhancing the defense with a few sharp spines extending from the hard carapace. In addition, the skin can secrete a toxic mucus (ostracitoxin) if the fish is placed under stress. The family contains only about two dozen species, less than half occurring in our area.

The family Tetraodontidae or puffers lack the armor of the trunkfishes, but the species have the ability to inflate themselves with water (or air if they are removed from the water) to balloon-like proportions, making them more difficult to swallow. They also secrete a toxin (tetrodotoxin) that is usually concentrated in the skin, gonads, or other internal organs. Japanese cooks are especially licensed to prepare these fishes for the table; even so, there are still a number of human fatalities in Japan due to puffer poisoning. Although the family is of respectable size (approximately ten genera and 120 species), only about nine or ten species in about four genera are found in our area. Puffers are circumtropical marine fishes although a few enter brackish or purely fresh waters.

The family Diodontidae contains fishes similar to the puffers that can also inflate themselves, but in addition they have bodies covered with strong spines so the inflated animal appears much like a pin-cushion. The teeth are fused into a solid beak (the puffers have their beaks separated in the middle). This is a small circumtropical marine family with less than two dozen species.

The family Molidae contains fishes with a very unusual shape. They look like they have a giant head with the body chopped off posteriorly. The dorsal and anal fins are opposite one another and located far back. These pelagic fishes eat jellyfishes along with small fishes and perhaps some algae. Only three species are included in this family, one of which (*Mola mola*) might reach a length of close to 4 meters with a weight of over 1,300 kilograms.

Index

Page numbers in **bold** face refer to illustrations

The following index contains entries for subject matter and illustrations contained in this book and its companion volumes, *Pacific Marine Fishes*, 1-7. Some of the names used in earlier volumes of this series, however, have been revised to reflect an updated or otherwise changed nomenclatural standing; all such names listed in text and index of these volumes are listed in this index but are referenced to show the revised identifications.

Malakichthys griseus, **1230**
Malakichthys wakiyai, **1230**
Man-O-War fishes, 416
Manta birostris, 1074, **1397**
Manta hamiltoni, **1942**
Mantas, 1074
Marine plotosid catfishes, 333
Marlins, 1257
Medialuna californiensis, **2014**, 2014
Megalaspis cordyla, **1058**
MEGALOPIDAE, 1041
Megalops cyprinoides, **1041**
Meiacanthus, 159, 1591
Meiacanthus atrodorsalis, **470, 1592, 1893**
Meiacanthus atrodorsalis oualensis, **470, 1593**
Meiacanthus grammistes, **469, 1335, 1594**
Meiacanthus herlihyi, **163**
Meiacanthus kamoharai, **164**
Meiacanthus mossambicus, **469, 637**
Meiacanthus sp., **1593**
Melichthys, 815
Melichthys indicus, **397**
Melichthys ringens (See *M. indicus*)
Melichthys vidua, **118, 120, 1628**
Mene maculata, 1167, **1168**
MENIDAE, 1167
Merinthe macrocephalus, **953**
Meuschenia skottowei, **121**
Microcanthus strigatus, 74, **76, 480, 1178**
MICRODESMIDAE, 172, 633
Micrognathus sp., **1970**
Micrometrus aurora, **2037**
Micrometrus minimus, 2034, **2037**
Microspathodon dorsalis, **2050**
Microstomus pacificus, **2176**
Midshipmen, 1821
Milkfish, 1044
Minous, 959
Minous monodactylus, **958**
Minous versicolor, **958**
Mirolabrichthys, 643
Mirolabrichthys dispar, **1472, 1473, 1476**
Mirolabrichthys evansi, **648, 650, 651, 742**
Mirolabrichthys tuka, **1383, 1474, 1475**
Mirolabrichthys tuka pascalus, **422**
Mobula diabolus, **1075**
MOBULIDAE, 1074
Mojarras, 917, 2003
Mola mola, **2182**, 2182
MOLIDAE, 2182
MONACANTHIDAE, 122, 819, 1351, 1905 (See also BALISTIDAE)
Monacanthus, 1905
Monacanthus chinensis (See *M. mylii*)
Monacanthus filicauda, **1355, 1905**
Monacanthus mosaicus, **399**
Monacanthus mylii, **400**
Monkfishes, 1069

MONOCENTRIDAE, 260, 1889
Monocentris gloriamaris, 260, 1889, **1889**
Monocentris japonica, 260, **273, 1158, 1159**
MONODACTYLIDAE, 74
Monodactylus argenteus, 74, **76, 312**
Monodactylus sebae, 74
Monotaxis, 664
Monotaxis grandoculis, **435, 642, 662, 663, 664-65, 1500, 1501**
Moonfishes, 74, 1167
Moorish idol, 75, 810
Moray eels, 260, 1403, 1945
Moringua microchir, **1409, 1410**
MORINGUIDAE, 1410
Morone saxatilis, **1972**
Morwongs, 251
Mudskippers, 172
Mugil cephalus, 313, **314, 315, 316**
MUGILIDAE, 313
MUGILOIDIDAE, 467, 477
Mullets, 313
MULLIDAE, 259, 739, 1461
Mulloides, 259, 739
Mulloides dentatus, **2010**
Mulloides flavolineatus, **739, 1461, 1465**
Mulloides pflugeri, **980**
Mulloides vanicolensis, **342, 980, 1460**
Mulloidichthys (= *Mulloides*)
Mulloidichthys auriflamma (See *Mulloides vanicolensis*)
Mulloidichthys dentatus (See *Mulloides dentatus*)
Mulloidichthys pflugeri (See *Mulloides pflugeri*)
Mulloidichthys samoensis (See *Mulloides flavolineatus*)
Mullus, 259
Mullus surmuletus, 1461
Muraena clepsydra, **1948**
Muraena lentiginosa, 1945, **1947**
Muraenesox cinereus, **351**
MURAENIDAE, 260, 1403, 1945
Mustelus henlei, **1938**
Mycteroperca prionura, **1983**
Mycteroperca rosacea, **1982, 1983**
Mylio latus, **437**
Mylio macrocephalus, **237, 438**
MYLIOBATIDAE, 1074, 1672
Myliobatis, 1672
Myliobatis tobijei, **1076**
Myoxocephalus polyacanthocephalus, **2157**
Myrichthys maculosus, **1949**
Myripristinae, 1966
Myripristis, 230, 689
Myripristis adustus, **233, 240**
Myripristis bowditchae, **1064**
Myripristris kuntee, **1694**
Myripristis leiognathus, **1936**, 1966, **1967**
Myripristis melanostictus, **688**
Myripristis murdjan, 230, **231, 232, 1064, 1450, 1694**
Myripristis pralinus, **341, 695, 1450**

Myripristis violaceus, **341, 694, 1449, 1450**
Myripristis vittatus, **1449**
Myripristis sp., **1617**
MYXINIDAE, 1933
Myxodagnus, 2076

N

Narke japonica, **1067**
Naso, 84, 89, 793
Naso brevirostris, **389, 807, 808, 1153, 1154, 1612**
Naso lituratus, 89, 90, **390, 804, 805, 806, 1155**
Naso lopezi, **389**
Naso unicornis, 89, **388, 807, 1152, 1153, 1154**
Naso sp., **808**
Naucrates, 423
Naucrates ductor, **1059**
Navodon ayraud, **1356**
Navodon modestus, **126, 1352**
Needlefishes, 329
Nematolosa japonica, **1047**
Nemateleotris decora, **1603**
Nemateleotris magnificus, 173, **176, 1011**
Nematistius pectoralis, **1998**
NEMIPTERIDAE, 666, 1493
Nemipterus, 666, 1493
Nemipterus bathybius, **439, 1294**
Nemipterus ovenii, **1303**
Nemipterus virgatus, **439, 1293**
Neoclinus blanchardi, **2082**
Neoclinus bryope, **163**
Neoditrema ransonneti, 335, **337**
Neoniphon, 230, 231, 689
Neoniphon laeve, **693**
Neoniphon operculare, **1452, 1453**
Neoniphon sammara, **233, 1062, 1452, 1688, 1689**
Neopercis aurantiaca (See *Parapercis aurantiaca*)
Neopercis multifasciatus (See *Parapercis multifasciata*)
Neopercis sexfasciata (See *Parapercis sexfasciata*)
Neopomacentrus azysron, **1727**
Neopomacentrus taeniurus, **724, 725**
Nexilarius concolor, **2041**
Nibblers, 433, 1163, 2014
Nibea albiflora, **1320**
Nibea goma, **1321**
Nibea mitsukurii, **1320**
Nicholsina denticulata, **2069**
Niphon spinosus, **544**
NOMEIDAE, 416, 1220
Nomeus gronovii, **417**
Notorynchus maculatus, **1934**
Novaculichthys taeniourus (See *Hemipteronotus taeniurus*)

O

Occella impi, 2165